IN JESUS' NAME

RECEIVE YOUR
SPIRITUAL

HEALING!

BY

Joletha Cobb

*NCCA Licensed Pastoral
Clinical Counselor*

IN JESUS' NAME
RECEIVE YOUR SPIRITUAL HEALING!

Published By Joletha Cobb Ministries

ISBN 978-0-6151-8085-4

Printed in the United States of America

TABLE OF CONTENTS

DEDICATION

This book is dedicated to my Heavenly Father above. Without His undying love, devotion, and healing in my life this book would not be possible. He has been the inspiration of this book and He wants me to share it with all of His beloved children. In Jesus' Name, He wants you to receive your spiritual healing so that you can be used as a vessel for His glory.

To my husband Hank, I would also like to dedicate this book for without his strength and support throughout my illness and my life; I would not have made it through. Thank you for all your support and love. You are the love of my life!

To my mother Bea, who has kept us grounded in the Word of God all of our lives. She is my source of inspiration and comfort. Thank you for always being there and I love you!

To my sister Charlotte, you are not only my sister but also my best friend. Thank you for your guidance and strength and for always being there for me, except for that leg iron thing!

To my children, Terry, Teramie, and Canaan I would like to say stay strong in Christ and I am proud of you all, just because you are my children and a gift from God.

To my grandchildren, Kierstin, Kaitlynn, Kaden, Emily Jolie', Matt, and Evan I would say to keep your eyes on Jesus and let Him lead you all of your lives. I love you very much. You are all the "apple of my eye".

FOREWORD

This book was written for the many believers and non-believers that may be suffering and needing a true spiritual healing. So many of God's precious children are suffering from spiritual sickness or spiritual brokenness due to past trauma or current trauma or unresolved past issues and don't know how to overcome and win back their spiritual health

Without our spiritual health we tend to take our eyes off of Jesus, the Word of God, and the things of God.

Spiritual sickness cripples us and blinds us to the blessings that God has for us in our lives. It can blind us to the calling that God has planned for us. We tend to start doubting God and wonder why He allows all of the bad things in our lives to occur. It prevents our emotional healing also. Our past traumas and pain have a great deal to do with our present spiritual condition.

We lose sight of our true purpose in this life and why the protection of God's hands has abandoned us.

This book is to give you a better understanding of spiritual sickness and how to obtain true spiritual and emotional healing. Spiritual healing can give us relief from all of the trials and turmoil we have gone through or may currently be going through. Spiritual healing can rid us of emotional ill health.

Many people have suffered abuse as children, or have had traumatic circumstances in their lives. They have a hard time letting go of the past and moving forward in life.

I will be talking to you about how to obtain your spiritual healing and conquer Satan's hold on you spiritually, emotionally, and physically. You will have true victory in Christ by breaking the bonds Satan holds on your life.

Do not live in bondage another day. Take back what is rightfully yours and gain back control of your life. This book is based on Scripture and what I believe is my true and accurate understanding of God's Word. I do urge readers of this book to pray for God's guidance for understanding of the Scriptures. Allow yourselves to be led by the Holy Spirit for true understanding of the Scriptures.

I pray this book will be a blessing to you and will aide you in your journey to spiritual healing. I pray this book will draw you nearer to Him as He desires for you to be.

"Draw nigh to God and He will draw nigh to you."

James 4:8

CHAPTER ONE

IN JESUS' NAME

This book is called "In Jesus' Name" for the purpose of recognizing what a great gift we have in Jesus. I couldn't possibly title this book as such without touching on the subject of how important Jesus' Name is and the power behind it.

God sacrificed Jesus for the sake of saving His precious children. He made a great sacrifice for us. Jesus was His only Son. If we think about it; would we or could we make this same sacrifice for someone else? I don't think we could or even would. God had such great love for us to make the most impossible task possible.

Who is Jesus? Almost everybody could tell you who Jesus is and what His ministry was while He was here on earth. Everyone has heard the Name Jesus. Does everyone know what the Name Jesus means? Does everybody know the power that is carried behind His Name? Probably not everybody.

Jesus is the Holy of Holies. He was God's only Son. He was both priest and king. Jesus was both human and divine and fitted to be the true savior of men. He is the wisdom and power of God unto salvation. His human side reaches down to our natures and sympathizes with us, and shows us that God knows all our feelings, weaknesses, our sorrows, and our sins. Jesus brings God to us. He is a divine, all powerful, and all loving Savior able and willing to defend us against our enemies, delivers us from all of our sins, and brings us to final victory. He is our brother and our friend. He is our comforter and our counselor.

Jesus had many names. He is called Jesus Christ. The name Jesus signifies "Savior." It is the Greek form "Johoshua" (Joshua). The name Christ signifies "anointed." In the New Testament the Name Christ is used as an equivalent to the Hebrew "Messiah" (anointed) in *John 1:41.*

John 1:41 He first found His own brother Simon, and said to him, "We have found the "Messiah" (which is translated, the Christ).

Other names for Jesus include "Lord," "King of Israel," "Emmanuel," "Son of David," and "Chosen of God," "The Almighty," and El Shaddiah." Jesus was also called Jehovah Jireh meaning Jehovah will see or provide. Jehovah means, "I am," and "The Eternal Living One." The name Jehovah Jireh was given to Jesus by Abraham when Jesus told Abraham to offer Isaac as a sacrifice.

No matter which name He is called, the Name of Jesus Christ holds much power.

When God sent His Son, Jesus, He gave Him a ministry. A ministry that would require Him to travel to all the lands and spread the Gospel and to teach to all that would listen about God and the chance for our salvation.

Jesus performed many miracles to show people about the blessed gifts God could offer them. He taught them about the chance to be saved and the harvest we would reap if indeed we received Jesus Christ as our Lord and Savior. He knew why He was here, to die for us. But after He died and rose again He did not leave us unprotected against Satan. He gave us the power of His Name. With using His Name requires
having great faith. Without this kind of faith using His Name is of no use. You must believe in the power of His Name.

Mark 11:23-24; So Jesus answered them and said to them, "Have faith in God. For assuredly I say to you, whoever says unto this mountain, "Be thou removed and be cast into the sea", and does not doubt in his heart, but believes in those things he says will be done, He will have whatsoever he says. Therefore I say to you, "Whatever things you ask when you pray, believe that you receive them, and you will have them".

We must believe when we pray. We must believe in the power of Jesus' Name. If we do, we can have whatsoever we ask.

Jesus gave us the power to use His Name in prayer.

John 14:14 Jesus said, "If you ask anything in My Name I will do it."

John 16:23 "Most assuredly I say to you, whatever you ask the Father in My Name He will give you."

Jesus provided a way for us even though He could not be with us here on Earth anymore. When we have need for something He will provide when we ask in Jesus' Name.

John 15:16 "You did not choose Me, but I chose you and appointed you that you should go and bear fruit and that your fruit should remain, that whatever you ask in My Name He may give you."

He chose US. But we have to choose HIM. We are to grow in maturity and bear much fruit and we can have whatsoever we ask: IN JESUS" NAME.

What gifts can we receive by using Jesus' Name?

Mark 16:16-18 says "He who believes and is baptized will be saved; but he who does not believe will be condemned. And these signs shall follow those who believe; In My Name they will cast out demons, they will speak new tongues, they will take up serpents, and if they drink anything deadly it will by no means harm them and they will lay hands on the sick and they will recover.

What a great blessing! What a gift from our Almighty Savior! Praise you Jesus!

To receive true spiritual healing the need for your faith in the power of Jesus' Name is of the utmost importance.

With each of the following chapters you read and the techniques you use, remember healing comes in the power of Jesus' Name, for without the power of Jesus nothing is possible.

Scripture: John 14:13 "And Whatever you ask in My Name, that I will do, that the Father may be glorified in the Son."

Prayer: Dear Heavenly Father, I thank you for the blessed gift of salvation you have provided for me. Father I thank you for providing your Son as a sacrifice in my place. Lord I pray you will give me new understanding as I read this book and you will help me strengthen my faith. Father I believe in the power of Jesus' Name and thank you for all the many gifts that come with it. You are truly an unselfish God and I praise you each day.

In Jesus' Name
Amen

CHAPTER TWO

SPIRITUAL SICKNESS

What is spiritual sickness? Spiritual sickness is when we have nothing left to give, spiritually, emotionally, and physically. Spiritual sickness is when we have allowed things of this world, such as abuse, depression, stress and much more to take the place of our spiritual peace, joy, and love. It has a way of crippling us to the point where it can prevent us from moving on in our lives. It inhibits our relationship with others, it inhibits us to be useful Christians, it can inhibit our relationship with God, and it can inhibit our salvation. It affects our bodies physically. It can cause us to suffer from depression, low self-worth, fear, anxiety, bitterness, anger, stress, chemical abuse, or a feeling of loneliness, and distress.

What can cause spiritual sickness? Many, many, many things can cause spiritual sickness. We all go through many trials and turmoil in our lives. You may have lost the life of a loved one, not only to death but you can lose a family member by abandonment or rejection, which can be just as traumatic, you may have gone through a tremendous amount of abuse as a child or an adult, or you may have wandered away from God. You may have endured a traumatic experience somewhere in your life that you are having trouble healing from. You may have depression, low self-confidence, or low self-worth. You may have guilt or shame about an event in your life. You may be suffering from anxiety or feeling that God has forsaken you. You may have encountered medical problems and are searching for your healing. You may have backslidden and sin has caused you to lose your spiritual health. Whatever the cause, it all comes down to the same thing: spiritual sickness.

Being an NCCA Licensed Pastoral Clinical Counselor, I will be giving you some tools to help you to overcome all of the causes I have mentioned above. With spiritual health comes a great deal of healing from the problems that may have caused your spiritual sickness. I will be discussing some techniques to help you overcome and reach your goal to spiritual healing, which will be a lot of work on your part: but very necessary to overcome pain you have endured and may still be enduring. You will be able to learn how to continue in your spiritual growth.

Your spiritual healing has to come from you and the allowance of God's help for you. Without God's help you will not make it through. The key to obtaining true spiritual healing is to reach down as far as you can in your spirit and be as honest as you can with yourself. You will have to understand and accept the true cause of your spiritual sickness.

Honesty with yourself is the key to true healing. It will be very difficult especially if the cause has been very traumatic for you. You may need a support person that is close to you such as a friend, family member, or spouse. You could also use your pastor as your support. God will be there to also be support for you.

You must also realize your value to Christ for spiritual healing. You are worth the healing from God. He can take away all your pain and give you comfort. Realize for yourself the value of your worth to God. This is very important.

I want you to be successful in reaching your goal for spiritual healing. I have faith in you and I want you to have faith in yourself.

In the next chapter we will be discussing how to identify the cause of your spiritual sickness. After each chapter there will be a prayer I would like for you to pray. These prayers will help you throughout the process. Use them over and over again. Also, read the Scriptures after each chapter in the Bible for true understanding as the Spirit leads you and read them over and over again.

There will also be worksheets for you to do. This is your homework. These worksheets will help you to understand the cause and the cure for spiritual sickness and how to work through it. Your homework is very important for you. It will give you continued understanding to your spiritual sickness and aide you in your healing.

Now, are you ready for success? Let's start the journey for your new life! Get excited about it! Look forward to living a life of healing from all of your pain you've had to deal with in your life, gaining a renewed spirit and a closer relationship with God. May God bless each of you with a new understanding of yourselves and spiritual healing for complete and total victory in Christ!

Scripture: "Is anyone among you suffering? Let him pray. Is anyone cheerful? Let him sing psalms. Is anyone among you sick? Let him call for the elders of the church, and let them pray over him, anointing him with oil in the name of the Lord. And the prayer of faith will save the sick, and the Lord will raise him up, and if he has committed sins, he will be forgiven."

James 5:13-15

Prayer: Father in Heaven,

I thank you for each new day you allow me. I am so thankful for your love and many blessings you have given me. Father, I pray today that you will open my eyes and my spirit for new understanding. Father I pray for spiritual healing for me. I pray for you to renew my spirit, Father. Draw me near to you and allow me to be honest with myself and face the things I need to face for true healing. I love you and I praise you for my healing. Thank you Father.

In Jesus' Name,
Amen

WORKSHEET

FIRST STEPS TO SPIRITUAL HEALING

Be honest with yourself.

Find a person for support if needed.

Keep an open mind.

As we search for a cause of your spiritual sickness, accept it openly, and allow yourself to work through it for total healing

Pray each day for new understanding.

Have faith in God for healing.

Be very vigilant in doing your homework

This will give you extra support and techniques for healing

Read the Scriptures after each chapter repeatedly.

CHAPTER THREE

IDENTIFYING THE CAUSE OF SPIRITUAL SICKNESS

In the last chapter we discussed some of the things that can cause spiritual sickness. They were loss of a loved one, whether by death, rejection, or abandonment, abuse as a child or adult, illness, sin, some traumatic event in your past, depression, low self-esteem or self-confidence, guilt or shame, bitterness, anxiety, anger, forsakenness, or there could be many other causes.

The secret to healing is to identify the cause of the problem. In physical healing a doctor has to determine the cause of the illness. They must talk to for your identification of your symptoms, they must run many tests, and they must come up with a diagnosis. They have to know what is causing the illness before they can cure it. It works the same way with spiritual and emotional healing. You have to know and identify what is creating the problem.

In identifying the cause you have to be very honest with yourself. For example, if you are angry with someone, it can affect your spiritual condition. If you have backslidden and are in sin you must be honest with yourself to be able to admit it. If the cause is due to trauma sometimes we will try to suppress or ignore our emotions to keep from dealing with them. It will always be there and it will always have an affect on your life and your spirit.

You must face these emotions before you can learn how to conquer them for you to receive spiritual healing. You must sometimes relive them in order to understand the pain they have caused. You may need to release your emotions of your trauma in order for it to pass and free you.

This can be very difficult. This is why I suggest for you to find someone who can give you the needed emotional support.

Identifying the cause is the first and most important step in spiritual healing. Once you can identify the cause you can then move forward and learn how to conquer the affects the cause has had on your life up to this point.

Identifying the cause is the secret to true freedom. Once you have the tools to face and conquer the cause, never again can it hold you in spiritual bondage. This is a very frightening part of gaining spiritual healing but it will be worth the victory of not allowing it to control you any longer. Satan holds God's people in bondage through their emotions and by physical illness. We have the power to release that bondage by the power of God's Word. We have to take back control of our lives and allow for God's protection through His Word.

Identifying the cause is the only way we will be able to face the demon that continues to control our lives. We have to get to the root of the problem before we will find true freedom and healing. Once we face that demon, never again can it hurt us.

Use the worksheet to help you identify the cause of your spiritual sickness. There may be more than one cause of your spiritual sickness. Write them down on the worksheet. Explain your answer by giving an example for each answer. In other words, for each cause write down what created the cause. Be very honest with yourself. Pray this prayer for strength and courage to move forward to freedom, healing, and victory.

Scripture: Isaiah 53:5 "For He was wounded for our transgressions, He was bruised for our iniquities. The chastisement for our peace was upon Him, and by His stripes we are healed."

Prayer: Oh my precious Heavenly Father,

Thank you Dear God for the courage and the strength to identify the cause of my spiritual bondage. Allow me Oh Lord to move into victory. Draw me near to you Lord and let me feel your loving and comforting presence throughout my healing. Thank you Lord for healing my spirit and giving me a renewed mind. Thank you for loving me and helping me to be a useful and victorious child of God!

In Jesus' Precious Name,
Amen

WORKSHEET

IDENTIFYING THE CAUSE

Choose the identifying cause or causes and explain your answer. Write down the event that caused it.

Anger (explain)

_____

_____

_____

Depression (explain)

_____

_____

_____

_____

Illness (explain)

_____

_____

_____

_____

Grief (explain)

_____
_____
_____
_____

Guilt or shame (explain)

_____
_____
_____
_____

Abuse (explain)

_____
_____
_____
_____

Anxiety (explain)_____

_____
_____
_____

Low self-esteem or self-confidence (explain)

_____
_____
_____
_____

Unforgiveness (explain) _____

_____
_____
_____

Fear (explain)

_____
_____
_____
_____

Addiction (explain) _____

_____
_____
_____

Loss of a loved one by death, rejection, or
abandonment. (explain) _____

_____
_____
_____

Other (explain) _____

_____
_____
_____
_____

CHAPTER FOUR

EMOTIONAL AND SPIRITUAL HEALING

The First Step of Spiritual and Emotional Healing

Emotional healing is just as important as spiritual healing. Without emotional healing you cannot have spiritual healing. When you go through a trial in your life it affects you emotionally first. It then affects your spirit and then can affect you physically with physical symptoms such as insomnia, weight loss, weight gain, over eating or no appetite at all, pain such as headaches or abdominal pain dizziness, or faintness. Your emotional and spiritual health can create many physical symptoms in your body and can cause illness.

To heal your body physically you must heal your emotions and your spirit. That is, if your illness is due to your emotional problem. Even with illness such as cancer and diabetes and other illnesses, some medical doctors and hospitals tend to not only treat your physical illness, they also give you emotional and spiritual treatment. You have to have spiritual re-conditioning in order to receive your healing.

You must have faith to obtain any sort of healing: physical, emotional, or spiritual. You must also have faith in your doctor and your nurses and most importantly faith in God. Without faith God cannot work. Without faith you can't receive healing. God works through our faith. We must have faith of God's power for spiritual healing.

To help your body heal you must have a positive attitude. Your mind has great control over the body. Without hope, faith, and a positive outlook on your illness you will have a more difficult time being healed. Our outlook on our illness will have great affect on our healing. You must desire to be healed and you must believe you are being healed. Your positive attitude will be a great asset to your healing.

In *2 Timothy 1:7* it talks about God's children having power and a **"sound mind".**

"For God has not given us a spirit of fear but of power and of love and of a "sound mind".

God desires His beloved children to be of **sound mind**; that means spiritually and emotionally. He desires for us to see ourselves as He sees us. He sees us as valuable, loveable, and forgivable. You must see yourself the same. You must have value, love, and forgiveness for yourself. If you don't value yourself then how can God have value for you?

Your self-worth is a major step in your healing. He sees us as loveable so then we must be able to see ourselves as loveable. We must have forgiveness for ourselves. No matter what we may have done in the past, God has forgotten it when you ask for His forgiveness. He remembers it no more. The problem occurs when we hang on to guilt and have a difficult time forgiving ourselves.

The very first step in achieving spiritual healing is faith in God and His promises as well as faith in yourself. You are worth the value He sees in you.

First you have to believe. You must believe in yourself, other people, and God. You have to believe that God exists and that He created you, loves you, and takes care of you. You must believe in God's Word. You must believe in Jesus Christ and that He came because of your sin and died for you. Without faith you cannot please God. You must believe in

YOURSELF.

Matthew 6:30-34 says, *"Do not worry saying, "What shall we eat?" or "What shall we drink?" or "What shall we wear?" For your Father in Heaven knows that you need all these things. But seek ye first the kingdom of God and His righteousness and all these things shall be added to you. Therefore do not worry about tomorrow, for tomorrow will worry about it's own things. Sufficient for the day is it's own trouble."*

Luke 17:5 and the apostles said to the Lord, "Increase our faith".

Romans 3:22 "Even the righteousness of God, through faith in Jesus Christ to all and on all who believe. For there is no difference <u>for all have sinned and fallen short of the kingdom of God."</u>

We have all fallen short. We have to give up our ideas of perfectionism and understand we cannot be perfect. There was only one perfect man and His name is Jesus. We cannot possibly be perfect. If we could, we would be like Jesus. We can never be like Jesus. We can only strive for His perfection. We must be satisfied with our strong points and continually work on our weak points. We have to have peace within ourselves and know that God loves us unconditionally.

Romans 5:12 "Therefore having been justified by faith we have peace with God through our Lord Jesus Christ through whom also we have access by faith into this grace in which we stand and rejoice in hope of the glory of God."

We have been justified by our faith. We can have peace with God through Jesus. It is by His grace we are made righteous. It is not something we can accomplish on our own but it comes only through the Father.

2 Timothy 4:7 "I have fought the good fight, I have kept the faith".

We must fight the good fight like Paul talked about in *2 Timothy 4:7* through our faith in God and we can win. With faith in God, He is on our side. He is all- powerful. We have the same power accessible to us by our faith. We only have to reach out and take it.

Hebrews 12:2 "Looking unto Jesus the author and finisher of our faith, who for the joy that was set before Him endured the cross, despising the shame, and has sat down at the right hand of the throne of God".

All of these verses talk about how faith affects you. Your faith has an affect on every area of your life. Paul in *2 Timothy* talked about fighting the good fight by keeping his faith.

You can all fight the good fight by having a strong faith in God. Keeping our faith strong is a fight in itself. It is easy to have faith in the good times but when things go wrong our faith wanes. We must learn to be able to keep our faith strong in good or bad times. If you can have faith in your earthly father who took care of you, how much more important is it to have faith in our Ultimate Father and Lord Jesus Christ?

We are not to worry about anything. What good does it do for us to worry about things we have no control of changing? Worrying is a very easy thing to do. It is hard not to worry but if we have no control over it anyway why not give it to God who does have control over it? We are to turn our troubles that we have no control of over to God. Allow Him to take care of it. He will do a much better job at it than us. Faith in knowing that God is working is the key that unlocks the door to Heaven.

Now recounting what I have talked about, the first and most important step to recovery and spiritual healing is faith. When you can have unwavering faith then comes the gift of healing.

Worship and Praise

The next and second step to spiritual healing is worship and praise. What is the reason for worship and praise? When we worship and praise God it draws us closer to Him. God delights in your praises. Everything we have, strength, power, energy, and fulfillment comes from God. Without God you have nothing. When you are in the act of worship and praise you turn your mind completely towards Him. You don't think about yourself or your problems.

Praise and worship are like therapy for your body. It releases all of your concerns and troubles as you concentrate upon God so your spirit can be edified. Taking our minds off of our problems and putting it onto God will give us the peace He has promised to us.

Praise strengthens our faith. Praise helps you to accept your situation, whether it changes or not. When you have faith in God completely you are releasing Him to work freely in your life so you can have victory over any situation.

When we praise and worship God it gives us a peace beyond understanding. We are giving ourselves to Him completely. When we are in the process of praise and worship we are yielding to His Word, we are opening our spirits up to Him and allowing Him to fellowship with us. The Lord loves and desires our praise and fellowship.

When you are down and you begin to praise and worship God you will have a peace unsurpassed by anything you have ever dreamed of. Praise and worship brings peace, joy, and increased faith into our lives. When we praise and worship God we are showing our thankfulness to Him. We are giving Him our love.

Psalms 22:3 says, *"God is Holy and that He is "enthroned" in the praises of Israel."*

Psalms 84:1, 2, 4 expresses the joy of worship. *"How lovely is Your tabernacle, O Lord of Hosts?" My soul longs, yes, even faints for the courts of the Lord; my heart and my flesh cry out for the living God…Blessed are those who dwell in Your house, they will still be praising You."*
John 4:23 "But the hour is coming and now is, when the true worshippers will worship the

Father in spirit and in truth. For the Father is seeking such to worship Him."

God so desires your praise and worship. The book of *Psalms 149* is a chapter on praise and worship. Spend time reading the book of Psalms. It will edify your spirit.

Psalms 150:6 says, *"Let everything that has breath praise the Lord".*

God inhabits the praises of His people. Take time to praise and worship Him each day. It will draw you closer to God, build your faith, and give you peace beyond understanding. It will edify your spirit, it will give you joy and peace in your in your life. It allows you to communicate with God and for God to communicate with you.

Prayer

The third step to spiritual healing is prayer. What does prayer have to do with spiritual healing or emotional healing?

A tremendous amount! How do we get our healing whether it is spiritual or physical? Well doctors help us to heal: but who works through the doctors? Doctors can help us to get our physical healing but doctors cannot help us get our spiritual healing. Doctors get their ability from God. God works through doctors. If God works through doctors then who gives us our healing? **GOD.**

We pray for God to heal us whether He works through doctors or on His own. But prayer without faith is useless. God cannot work without our faith in Him.

Prayer strengthens our faith. Just as we need physical care so do we need spiritual care?

The human body is divided up into 3 parts: Mind, body, and soul. Our mind is the thinking process or the brain part of our bodies. The brain tells our bodies what we want them to do. We all know what our body is. It is the shell of our frame. It is also the temple of the Holy Spirit. Our soul is our spirit. Our spirit is how God communicates with us. We enter God's presence through prayer. When our spirits are weak then so is our prayer life and our relationship with God.

Spiritual healing has to come from God according to our faith, our praise and worship to God, and through prayer. Prayer is not used to only ask God to bless us with things of this world. Yes, He says in His Word to ask and it shall be given to you but He doesn't want us to pray to Him only to ask for things. He wants us to fellowship with Him under any circumstances. He wants to draw closer to us and for us to draw closer to Him. He wants us to have a true relationship with Him.

Prayer is time spent with God and how He fellowships with us. Prayer is talking to God. When we pray we are submitting our wills to Him allowing Him to work. It is spending time with God and we are to be still and listen to Him. When we surrender our spirits to Him, He enters our spirit. We learn and draw upon His wisdom.

When we pray we are learning about God and getting to know Him just as we would by talking to other people.

The Word says in *1 Thessalonians 5:17 "Pray without ceasing"*. Does this mean we spend all of our time praying?
Yes, we cannot only pray verbally but spiritually. We should include Him in the decisions we make in every aspect of our daily lives. We pray for wisdom about every decision we have to make in our lives. If we allow Him to be included by praying constantly we cannot fail. Praying without ceasing is an ongoing praise, worship, and prayer that we do physically and mentally.

The Word says we can ask for help.

In *Matthew 7:7* it says, *"Ask and you shall receive, seek and you shall find, knock and the door will be opened to you"*.

When we do not ask for God's help and try to do everything for ourselves we often fail. We get too comfortable about handling everything on our own.

When we pray we should start off by telling God how much we love Him. We should give Him praise and thank Him for the blessings He has already given to us and for who He is.

When we pray we need to pray for others as well as ourselves. We need to be specific in our prayers and pray until the answer comes. But prayer is only answered through our faith. Without faith we can accomplish nothing.

The more time we spend in prayer the healthier and stronger we become spiritually. Spiritual healing cannot occur without prayer.

Prayer also allows us to talk to God about anything. He is the ultimate Counselor. We can talk to Him about anything without judgment. When we go through trials and tribulations we need to be able to talk about it and with God that is always possible.

Most of us only pray to God when we are in a crisis. God does not want to be used as a temporary hero. He wants to be our hero all the time.

Start each day off in prayer and throughout the day and notice the change in how your day goes. It will release a great deal of stress from us when we allow Him to take care of our lives. We are not strong enough to handle all of our problems on our own. We sometimes find ourselves at the end of our rope, frustrated, angry, and questioning God. Allow God to be your Hero every day. Let Him take those worries off of you and let Him take care your problems. With worrying comes stress. With stress come physical problems. Give your stress to God. Allow Him to take over.

Imagine what the world would be like without stress and worry. We can have that. Give it all to God. We can live a stress-free life when we allow our faith in God to take the place of our worry and stress. Pray without ceasing through out the day. Know that God desires for you to be stress free and He wants you to depend on Him for your needs.

John 14:14 "Jesus said if you ask anything in My Name and I will do it."

Matthew 21:22 "And whatever things you ask in prayer, believing, you will receive."

<u>BELIEVE</u> and you will **receive.**

Scripture: 1 Thessalonians 5:17 "Pray without ceasing."

Prayer: My Dearest Heavenly Father,

I love you with all of my heart and spirit. You are truly a holy and powerful God. Thank you Lord Jesus for the many blessings you have bestowed upon me. I praise you and I thank you. Father help me to be the person you have called me to be. I will learn to pray without ceasing as your Word has instructed. Strengthen my spirit so I can be what your divine plan calls for me to be. I surrender my spirit to you, oh God, for complete healing. Your Word says to ask for whatever I desire and believe and you will do it. Thank you Father, for your spiritual, emotional, and physical healing. I worship and praise you for you are worthy to be praised.
In Jesus' Name
Amen.

WORKSHEET

EMOTIONAL AND SPIRITUAL HEALING

Strengthen your faith each day through prayer and repeat *Luke 17:5,* And the apostles said to the Lord, "Increase our faith."

Worship and praise God throughout each day. Repeat *Psalms 22:3 "But You are holy, enthroned in the praises of Israel".*

Pray without ceasing.

Read *Ephesians 1:3-14.* Read *2 Samuel 22:2-51.* Read *Psalms 8: 19* and *27.*

Repeat *1 Thessalonians 5:17, "Pray without ceasing," every day."*

Set your alarm every morning 15 to 20 minutes earlier than usual and spend that time in prayer. Make prayer the first thing you do every morning. Pray throughout the day.

Make a list of your worries and see in your mind's eye physically handling this list over to Jesus. Pray that God will take care of these problems and pray for strength to no longer worry about these problems.

CHAPTER FIVE

SPIRITUAL GROWTH

Spiritual growth is very important for maintaining spiritual healing. When we become new believers we are still babes in Christ. We don't know as much about the Bible or God as a mature believer would. We have to learn everything anew. We must strive to become closer to God and learn about Him as much as possible. When we are babes in Christ we are immature Christians but when we strive for spiritual growth we become more mature.

For spiritual healing to occur we must grow and mature in our spirits. Spiritual growth is a developmental process that allows us to grow and perfect us to be Christ-like. It works the same way as the development process of a child. We must be able to go through the process and allow for it to mature us. The more we read the Bible, pray to God, and give Him praise and worship for edification of our spirits the more mature we will be as Christians. God does not want us to remain babes in Christ. He desires for us to become mature Christians to use us in His ministry. Becoming mature in Christ involves obedience to the Word of God and giving us the qualities of Jesus.

We cannot grow spiritually only by our own works: it is also by the works of God. We must allow Him to work through our spirit to perfect us His way. When we try to perfect our spirituality on our own, it can backfire on us. We do not have the knowledge of Christ to know how to grow spiritually. We grow through His power according to His will.

This does not mean that we sit back and do nothing to help us grow spiritually mature. Spiritual maturity comes through **our faith, our praise** **and worship, and our prayers**.

We must open ourselves up to Him; allow Him to mold us while being obedient to God. Spiritual growth is a process. To help ourselves grow spiritually we must get alone with God. We need to have solitude with God. Even Jesus had to have solitude with God. He had to pray to His Father for strength, comfort, and instruction.

Mark 1:32 "Now in the morning, having risen a long while before daylight, He went out and departed to a solitary place; and there He prayed".

Being alone with God allows us to hear God. When we are still in prayer with God He speaks to our spirit.

Next, we need to meditate on the Scripture. Meditation gives us time to understand the Word of God and to renew our minds. Meditation aids in the renewing of our minds.

Romans 12:2 "And do not be conformed to this world, but be transformed by the renewing of your mind that you may prove what is that good and acceptable and perfect will of God."

Silence and prayer, worship and service are examples of practices that need to be in our daily lives.

Attending church regularly helps us to grow spiritually. We not only learn about the Word of God but it gives us fellowship with God and other believers so we can share, celebrate, and remain strong in the Lord.

Every experience we go through in life; through each trial, allows us to grow spiritually. When we go through certain trials in our lives it makes us stronger for the next trial. It gives us strength and builds our faith, and most importantly, it allows us to mature spiritually. It allows us to understand how much God loves us, and how He helps us through each trial. We never go through these trials alone. He carries us through each one.

John 16:7 "Nevertheless I tell you the truth. It is to your advantage that I go away; for if I do not go away, the Helper will not come to you; but if I depart, I will send Him to you

Jesus made provision for us. He made sure that when He could no longer be with us physically the way He was with His disciples, but that He would send us a helper to always be here to help us through our trials. This is not to say that Jesus is not always there for us but the Holy Spirit is how He communicates with us. The Holy Spirit is within us.

God does not want us to live in bondage of the trials Satan puts upon us. He wants us to live as free children of God. He has made provision for us. He has adopted us into His family. We are heirs of God and joint heirs with Christ.

Romans 8: 15-17 "For you did not receive the spirit of bondage again to fear, but you received the Spirit of adoption by whom we cry out "Abba Father". The Spirit Himself bears witness with our spirit that we are children of God, and if children then heirs-heirs of God and joint heirs of Christ if indeed we suffer with Him, that we may also be glorified together."

This is a tremendous statement. We are adopted children of God being made joint heirs with Christ! Praise the Lord! We don't suffer alone. The Holy Spirit bears witness with our spirit.

With each new trial brings new testimonies in our lives for God's glory. We don't care to go through these trials but we should welcome them for the strengthening of our spirit and for the glory of God.

Scripture: Romans 12:1-2 "I beseech you therefore brethren by the mercies of God, that you present your bodies a living sacrifice, holy, acceptable to God, which is your reasonable service."

Prayer: Dear Father in Heaven,

Thank you for sending me your Helper to be with me during my trials. Help me to grow in your Word so that I may reach Christian maturity. Help me to overcome the bondage of Satan over my life and accept each new trial as a blessing for my spiritual health. I praise you and I worship you. I glorify your name.

In Jesus' Name,
Amen.

WORKSHEET

SPIRITUAL GROWTH

Spend at least 10 minutes or more alone with God in prayer each day. Write down what you received out of your solitude with God.

_____
_____
_____
_____
_____
_____
_____

Meditate on the Scriptures you have read each day. Write down what you received.

_____
_____
_____
_____
_____

Find a church if you don't already attend one and start attending regularly.

CHAPTER SIX

THE HOLY SPIRIT

Who is the Holy Spirit? The Holy Spirit was sent to us by Jesus, when He had to go to the Father. He was sent to us to be a Helper to us when Jesus could not be here on earth anymore for us. He is here as a way for us to communicate to God. He is here as our protector, to edify us, and to keep our faith strong. To help us obtain true spiritual healing we have to be willing to allow the Holy Spirit to enter our spirit.

When Jesus rose again He promised His disciples that although He was leaving, He was not abandoning them. He says in:

John 14: 16-18 "And I will pray to the Father and He will give you another helper, that He may abide with you forever-the Spirit of Truth-when the world cannot receive because it neither sees Him nor knows Him; but you know Him, for He dwells with you and will be with you. I will not leave you orphans; I will come to you."

Here He is saying that the Holy Spirit is in us and we will never be alone. We have to allow Him to enter us.

John 16:7 "Nevertheless I tell you the truth. It is to your advantage that I go away, for if I do not go away, the Helper will not come to you, but if I depart I will send Him to you."

The Holy Spirit is our counselor and our mentor. The Holy Spirit is always with us prompting us, maturing us, and guiding us to maturity.

John 16:13 "However, when He the Spirit of truth comes, He will guide you into all truth; For He will not speak on His own authority, but whatever He hears He will speak; And He will tell you things to come."

He helps us through many challenges we face. He fills us to overflowing, gives us eternal peace, builds our faith, empowers us, and teaches us.

John 14:17-26

The Holy Spirit intercedes for us to the Father.

Romans 8:26 "Likewise the Spirit helps us with our weaknesses. For we do not know what we shall pray as we ought, but the Spirit Himself makes intercession for us with groanings, which cannot be uttered."

We must allow ourselves to be led by the Holy Spirit on a daily basis. When we do this we are filled to overflowing with peace, faith, and joy.

The Father speaks to us through the Holy Spirit. This is how He communicates to us and also how we can communicate to Him. The Holy Spirit prays to the Father on our behalf.

With the Holy Spirit come many powerful gifts.

1 *Corinthians 12:4-11 "There are diversities of gifts, but the same Spirit. There are differences of ministries, but the same Lord. And there are diversities of activities, but it is the same God who works all in all. But the manifestation of the Spirit is give to each one for the profit of all, for the one is given the word of wisdom through the Spirit, to another the word of knowledge from the same Spirit, to another faith by the same Spirit, to another the gifts of healings by the same Spirit, to another the working of miracles, to another prophecy, to another discerning of spirits, to another different kinds of tongues, to another the interpretation of tongues."*

These gifts are freely ours. We may receive one or two of these gifts or we may receive all of these gifts. He gives us the same power Jesus has. We use these many gifts for ourselves and to help others. We can have and use these gifts in Jesus' Name. The Holy Spirit works through us with these many gifts. These gifts not only help others but they are here to help us.

All these gifts can be ours by allowing the indwelling of the Holy Spirit into our spirit. Spiritual healing comes through the Holy Spirit. With His help we can overcome many obstacles in our lives. We can have the peace, joy, love, and comfort of the Holy Spirit flowing from our spirits. What true spiritual healing!

The Holy Spirit is our protector, comforter, our convictor, our guide, and our encourager. He is ever present in our lives.

God loves us enough to never leave us nor forsake us. He made sure that when Jesus had to go home to Heaven, that He provided us with our helper, the Holy Spirit, to always be with us.

Scripture: 1 Corinthians 3:16 "Do you not know that you are the temple of God and that the Holy Spirit dwells in you?

Prayer: Father in the Name of Jesus,

I thank you for sending your helper, the Holy Spirit to dwell in my life. Father I pray you will fill me with the presence of the Holy Spirit. Fill me with your unending love, peace, and joy. Allow me to receive the gifts of the Holy Spirit so that I may be used as a vessel for your glory. I thank you and I praise you blessed Jesus for all you have given on my behalf. I love and praise you.

In Jesus' Name,
Amen.

WORKSHEET

THE HOLY SPIRIT

Read *John 14:16-18, Luke 12:12,* and *Acts 2:1-4*

Pray the above prayer for receiving the gift of the Holy Spirit.

Allow the Holy Spirit become a part of your spirit.

If you have already been baptized with the Holy Spirit, write down the gifts you have received from Him.

CHAPTER SEVEN

GOD'S PROMISES

Up to this point we have talked about spiritual sickness, identifying the cause, healing, spiritual growth and the Holy Spirit. After reading each of these chapters how ready are you for receiving your spiritual healing? You may be thinking, "How do I know that all of these things will give me spiritual healing?"

In this chapter we will be discussing God's promises. A promise is a guarantee that something will happen. Many people make promises but don't necessarily keep them. It is hard to trust a person who has broken their promises in the past. But God keeps His promises.

Promises can be immediate or not immediate. There are short-term promises and long-term promises.

God's first promise to us involved the flood. God promised Noah and his sons in;

Genesis 9:8-12 saying, *"And as for me, behold, I establish My covenant with you and with your descendents after and with every living creature that is with you…. never again shall all flesh be cut off by a flood to destroy the earth? And God said, "This is a sign of the covenant which I make between you and me and every living creature that is with you for perpetual generations. I set my rainbow in the cloud, and it shall be a sign of the covenant between Me and the earth."*

Every time we see a rainbow in the clouds, this is a reminder of God's promise. Every promise God ever made has been fulfilled. In *Genesis 15:4* He promised Abraham and Sarah with a son.

"And behold the Word of the Lord came to him saying, "this one shall not be your heir but one who will come from your own body shall be your heir."

In *Genesis 15:5* God said,

"Look toward Heaven and count the stars if you are able to number them and He said, "So shall your descendents be".

He then promised Abraham the Promised Land flowing with milk and honey in *Genesis 15:7.* The Bible is full of God's promises. His promises to us are also fulfilled.

In *Joel 2:32* God says, *"That whosoever calls on the name of the Lord shall be saved"*.

Sending His beloved Son Jesus who died on OUR behalf for OUR sins fulfilled that promise.

In *Matthew 28:20* God promises His presence with His people,

"I am with you always, even to the end of the age."

2 Corinthians 1:20 says, *"For all the promises of God are Yes, and in Him."*

When we get in the dark times it is hard to stand on God's promises. We have to stand on the Scripture before we can see the light at the end of the tunnel. We must meditate on God's Word, even though we cannot see God we have to stay strong in faith and believe in God's promises.

Mark 11:24 "Whatever things you ask when you pray believe that you receive them and you shall have them."

Whatsoever we pray we shall have it. God fulfills His every promise He has made to us. We have to believe in these promises and reach out and take them for our own. Stand on the faith of God's promises and pray for your spiritual healing. **In Jesus' Name** we shall have whatsoever we desire. Whatsoever we desire!

We must ask for God to fulfill His promises in our lives. If we have not it is because we ask not. God can fix any problem we endure in our lives.

He can give us the strength to stand on His Word. Put your faith in God's promises for total victory and your spiritual healing. He promises us happiness, joy, peace, protection, comfort, and prosperity. Reach out and claim the promises of God. It is His will to see us succeed!

Scripture: 2 Peter 1:4 "By which have been given to us exceedingly great and precious promises that through these you may be partakers of the divine nature."

Prayer: Precious Heavenly Father,

Lord you have given me many blessings in my life. I worship you and praise you for prayer for you deserve my praise. Father although I am not worthy you have kept your many promises to me. Thank you Lord Jesus for giving up your life for mine. Father make me strong in spirit and in truth. Strengthen me O Lord to have spiritual healing Father. I want to be the child of God that you want me to be. Thank you for healing me emotionally, physically, and spiritually. I love you dearly.

In Jesus' Name,
Amen

WORKSHEET

GOD'S PROMISES

Write out two Scriptures of God's promises on paper and tape it to your mirror. Each time you look in the mirror read those scriptures, especially in the morning while getting dressed for the day.

On the same paper as you wrote the Scriptures write down a promise you want God to fulfill in your life and read it at the same time as you read the Scriptures and give thanks for it.

CHAPTER EIGHT

RECOVERING FROM ABUSE

Now it is time to get into the meat of this book. Our spiritual healing can be hindered by many things. We will be discussing different hindrances that you may be suffering from and give some actual counseling techniques for each.

Due to the evil world we live in, many people go through some form of abuse. It may have been physical, emotional, or verbal abuse as a child or the result of living in a household with domestic violence, rape, beatings, or trauma from another source in their life.

Whatever the abuse, it is just as traumatic. Any form of abuse is traumatic to us physically, emotionally, and spiritually. It can rob you of your joy, your health, your peace, your self-confidence, your trust, and your self-esteem. You may suffer from fear or anger.

Any form of abuse without counseling from a professional could cause Post Traumatic Stress Disorder. PTSD is an emotional problem that is caused by some traumatic event in your life and you are unable to work through it or overcome it. It affects you daily. It can literally cripple you and your life.

How do you ever live through these traumas and be able to function normally? How do you regain your spiritual health?

As an NCCA Licensed Pastoral Clinical Counselor I have counseled with many people with PTSD who have gone through abuse. I will be giving you some techniques for helping you to cope, overcome, heal, and take back control of your life.

The first thing to remember about abuse is **it is not your fault.** You must not lay the blame on yourself. You did nothing wrong. Release those thoughts from your mind. Get comfort in knowing you are not the only one who has suffered from abuse as a child or as an adult. Your abuse is the fault of the abuser. Those that abuse, suffer from very low self-worth. They have no confidence in themselves. They have no control of their own lives. They feel that they must have that control over their lives. They take that control by controlling or abusing someone else. It is never about you or who you are: it is never a personal thing against you; it is a very personal thing within the abuser.

If you have trouble removing the blame from yourself please read the chapter on self-esteem. Trauma from abuse can create many emotional and physical problems. It can cause depression, insomnia, over-sleeping, weight loss or weight gain, fear, unforgiveness, anger, bitterness, anxiety, and guilt or shame.

I will be discussing techniques for each of these in following chapters.

The first thing I would recommend if you haven't done so already is if you have any of the symptoms above, you many need to see a doctor. Your doctor can prescribe you some medications to help ease some of these symptoms.

Trauma from your past can affect everything in your life. It can affect your relationships with others in the future. It can affect your relationship with God. It prevents you from living a normal well-balanced life. Obtaining counseling for abuse is very important.

Trauma is not the only thing that causes anger, depression, anxiety, fear, or any of the symptoms mentioned above. We can have any of these symptoms, either one or the other, or one or more symptoms together, due to other problems in our lives. We will be discussing all of these symptoms individually in future chapters.

God wants His children to be healthy. He never intended for you to have bad things happen to you.

He loves you very much. But God takes the bad things that Satan does to us and uses it for the good.

When we go through trials we become stronger. It builds our faith. It gives you the experience and knowledge to handle each trial in your life. We gain strength to handle the next crisis. We go through trials to gain Christian maturity. Without Christian maturity God cannot use us in His ministry. God wants us to grow and have our spiritual health to use us in His divine plan. Spiritual healing comes only through God and the Holy Spirit. You are a precious child of God and He desires you to be healthy physically, spiritually, and emotionally.

When we meditate on God's Word we can overcome the many trials that Satan throws our way. Our thought process can greatly affect us emotionally. It determines what our future will be like. Negative thoughts do not promote healing in our lives. It can rub on us like sandpaper and can keep us from obtaining the peace and joy that God desires for us. When we think negative thoughts, we refer to this as faulty thinking. When we think negatively usually the negative will come true. When we think positively, usually the positive will come true. The positive things we put in our minds and spirit will usually overcome the negative things. When we learn to replace our faulty thinking we can control the thoughts that we think about.

Every person has a will and an imagination. Our will is what we decide to do. It is our choice to do whatever we choose to do within our will. Our imagination is our thought process. When we think the worst we will get the worst. The imagination has much power over our will. The imagination will usually win over the will. Compulsive thoughts that run through our minds will take over our minds completely. If we let them we will dwell on them constantly.

They can drive us crazy if we let them. We have control over our thoughts. We can choose to think negative things or we can choose to think positive things. Either way the imagination will usually win over our will. If we learn to replace the negative thoughts with a counter thought, a positive thought, then, when we put that into our imaginations then it will usually win over the will. Changing the things we put into our imagination will win over our will. The first thing we will learn is how to think with our imagination for successful healing.

We can control a great deal of what occurs in our lives by what we think and put into our imagination. Have you ever been afraid? Let's say, for example, that a burglar came into your house in the middle of the night and walked in on you. The burglar left without harming you but now you have a fear that this will happen again. You will begin to hear things in the middle of the night thinking that it is the burglar again when in fact it was the cat scratching on the door to come in. I am not saying do not be cautious, but when something occurs in our lives we tend to think it will happen again so the fear consumes us and will literally control how we function in our lives. This is where we learn to take control over our thoughts so that they don't control us.

If the imagination usually wins over the will then whatever we think affects our lives.

Proverbs 23:7 says, **"For as a man thinketh in his heart so he is."**

As we think so are we. We allow our imagination to win over our will. When we have negative thoughts, they usually come to past. With each of the next few chapters we will be using this approach. We must learn to put the positive thoughts into our imagination and see ourselves in the positive. Victorious over all that Satan puts upon us. Changing our mind-set is an important step in our spiritual healing. When you understand how much control you have over your imagination you can come out victorious in most circumstances.

Trauma from abuse can take a very long time to heal. Some may never heal from it. It is always in the forefront of their minds. They can't seem to put it away in their minds. Those that suffer from abuse must be able to confront the fact that the abuse occurred, work through it, and file it away. Our brains cannot file it away if we haven't acknowledged it yet.

If you have been having trouble storing away the memories of abuse you may want to seek the help of a professional.

I will be giving you some techniques to help you to confront the abuse and help you find peace within yourself. A very important thing I would like to mention is that I will be issuing homework; you must be able to follow these techniques and do your homework. The homework will help if you put your mind to doing it. It is a very important step in the process of healing.

I will be giving you some techniques to help you overcome the feelings of helplessness that comes from trauma. These techniques will help you to take back the control that you lost from the abuse.

Please take these homework assignments very seriously. It will be difficult for you at first but with each day it should be less and less difficult.

My prayers are with you. I have faith in you to overcome because you are a precious child of God and it is He who will be right beside you all the way. Depend on Him for comfort and talk to Him daily for strength. Allow Him to be a very big part of your therapy. He can be the strength you need to overcome. Good luck on this journey. Again, find a support person for you to be able to talk to.

This will be the hardest part of your journey and to be able to overcome you will need to learn how to change your faulty thinking. Work on these techniques every day.

Allow yourself to release your emotions, as this will help you to heal. Don't be afraid to express your inner most emotions. God is right beside you. Don't be afraid. He will give you the comfort you need and the strength to overcome. My prayers are with you each day!

Scripture: Psalms 23:7, "For as a man thinketh in his heart so he is."

———————●———————

Prayer: Father in Heaven,

I praise you and I thank you for being my Heavenly Father. Thank you for making me and molding me to maturity. Father, I pray you will fill my mind with positive thoughts O Lord. Teach me Lord how to keep my thoughts positive to gain control over the circumstances in my life. Thank you Lord for your Word as a guide for my life. Help me to allow you to guide me with Your Word. Give me complete understanding and peace of mind. Thank you for your protection and no weapon formed against me shall prosper.
I love you and I praise you for my spiritual healing.

In Jesus' Name,
Amen

WORKSHEET

RECOVERING FROM ABUSE

Release all blame from yourself. It was not your fault. God does not blame you. He loves you and you need to love yourself. Read **_John 3:16_**

Write down on paper all of your feelings about the trauma or abuse you suffered through. Write for 15 minutes a day without stopping or thinking about what you are writing. Just write the first thing that comes into your mind. Do this for 2 weeks every day.

After 2 weeks have passed and you have written for 15 minutes a day then I want you to write a letter to the one who abused telling them how you are feeling about the abuse and how you felt as the abuse was in progress. Tell them how it has affected your life. Anything you want to tell them, write down. Let them know about the anger you have. If you know this person you can either send it to them or if you choose not to, then burn the letter. If you don't know the person who abused you then burn the letter or bury it in your yard as a way of saying it is over. Burning the letter releases you. The letter releases your ability needed to move on with your life.

Now this is the hard part. Forgive the abuser and yourself.

Forgiveness is not releasing the abuser of responsibility; it mainly helps you move on without living your life with the anger that comes with abuse. You will never forget but you need to forgive to gain back control of your life. If not, the abuser will always have control over you. Read the chapters on forgiveness, anger, depression, guilt or shame, grief, and restoration. These chapters will help you with each emotion you are suffering through.

Read *Philippians 4:13 "I can do all things through Christ Who strengthens me"* **every day.**

Pray every day for God's help. He will give you peace, and the strength to overcome, heal your spirit, and live again.

Fill out this worksheet, being very honest with yourself so you can learn how to control your thoughts. Use this worksheet to help you learn to change your thought process.

TECHNIQUE FOR CORRECTING THOUGHTS

Write down your thoughts in the left column and list the correction of the belief on the other. Do this whenever you have negative thoughts.

EX: Negative thought: I can't stand being alone.
Correction answer: I can stand difficulties, as I have in the past, I just don't like them.

Negative Thought	Corrected Thought

Technique For Changing Thought Patterns:

Ask yourself if you deeply desire to change.

You have to come to a place of being able to say,
"God, I do not want to have the kind of thought
life I have been having. I want to be rid of negative
images. They have created a barrier between you
and me. I want the thoughts and images you have
for me. Help me to use my imagination and
thought life in such a way that I can grow, mature,
help others more, and bring glory to you.

Pray for the desire to be rid of the old pattern of
thinking. Ask Jesus to come into your thought life
and allow the Holy Spirit into the depths of your
imagination, to bring to light the images or
thoughts that are creating a barrier.

During this prayer time, when a troublesome
thought or image comes to mind see yourself
taking it in your hands and giving it to Jesus.

Some people find it helpful as they pray to lift one
hand to the head, place the thought in your hand,
and then reach forward and place it in Jesus'
outreached hands. The physical movement along
with the prayer has a greater sense of reality to it
and strengthens their motivation.

This type of praying takes time and often needs to
be repeated for each image or thought that
emerges. This is not to say that these thoughts will

never return, but now you will be able to confront them in a new way.

Ask God for clearness of thought and direction. Use your God-given power of imagination to bring a change in your life and bring glory to you.

CHAPTER NINE
FORGIVENESS

Another important step in spiritual healing is forgiveness.

You must again identify the cause to spiritual sickness. If your spiritual sickness is due to unforgiveness of someone who may have harmed you in the past you must be able to open your spirit and forgive. We can also be angry with God due to an illness or the loss of a loved one or many other reasons.

Forgiveness does not mean we have to forget nor does it release the responsibility of the person you are upset with. Forgiveness is a sacrifice we make for ourselves. Un-forgiveness can become a disease. It can affect our physical and emotional health, our spiritual health, even our salvation. Forgiveness is very difficult to do but not impossible. It is necessary for our spiritual healing.

Unforgiveness does not affect the person you are angry with: unforgiveness only affects us. Unforgiveness causes bitterness, anger, resentment, and hate. It poisons our spirits with each passing day. It affects us daily. We have to change the unforgiveness, hatred, anger, and bitterness, to love, compassion, and caring emotions. Forgiveness is a continuing process that we have to do on a daily basis. We cannot just forgive someone in one day; it is an ongoing process. We are canceling a debt that someone owes. Forgiveness is realizing and seeing the good side of things instead of the bad.

You don't deny that you have been hurt; you just don't allow it to affect you anymore.

Next, you must try to look at the other person involved from their viewpoint for understanding. Writing down your options and your forgiveness or telling someone will help you to hold on to your forgiveness. Holding on to your forgiveness may require daily forgiveness. It doesn't go away immediately and often takes time and great effort.

Jesus forgives us each and every day. He has to forgive us over and over again.

Matthew 6:12 says *"And forgive us our debts as we forgive our debtors"*.

No one in this world can be perfect; Jesus has to continually forgive us. He forgives us on a daily basis. As soon as we ask for forgiveness He remembers it not more. He expects us to do the same. Un-forgiveness can also affect our salvation.

Mark 11:25 "And whenever you stand praying if you have anything against anyone, forgive them, that your Father in Heaven may also forgive your trespasses. But if you do not forgive, neither will your Father in Heaven forgive your trespasses."

Our Father can't forgive us unless we can forgive others.

Luke 6:37 "Judge not and you shall not be judged, Condemn not, and you shall not be condemned. Forgive and you shall be forgiven."

There are many Scriptures in the Word on forgiveness.
Forgiveness is a must for us to enter into the gates of Heaven. Remember Jesus cannot forgive us if we don't forgive others.

Forgiveness releases us of the anger and wrath that destroys our spirits. Unforgiveness can keep us from physical and spiritual healing and from having a close relationship with Christ. It puts up a wall between you and God. The longer we allow un-forgiveness to continue the longer it will take us to forgive.

Now that you see the importance of forgiveness, pray and ask God to help you with your un-forgiveness of others. This will release you for complete healing spiritually. Your emotions will change, the anger will leave, and your life will be happier when you forgive. **Do it for YOU**.

Scripture 1 John 1:9 "If we confess our sins He is faithful and just to forgive us our sins and to cleanse us from all righteousness

Prayer: My Precious Lord,

You have blessed me many times and I thank you for accepting me as a child of God. I thank you Jesus for your forgiveness of my sins continuously Father. Even though I am not perfect you have accepted me anyway. Thank you for giving your life for me. Help me to have a forgiving heart. Give me spiritual healing through my forgiveness of others. Lord I forgive all those that may have harmed me in the past. Allow me to be free from the bondage of un-forgiveness. Thank you for loving me and accepting my imperfect ways.

In Jesus' Name,
Amen.

WORKSHEET

FORGIVENESS

Write a letter to the person or persons you need to forgive. You may send it to them or you may decide not to. It is better if you tell the person that you have forgiven them.

Tell someone that you have forgiven the one with whom you are upset.

Each morning make a conscious choice to forgive the one you are angry with again and on a daily basis until all the feelings of negative emotion toward this person has diminished.

Read the following Scriptures on forgiveness: ***Romans 12:19, Luke 6:37, Luke 17:3*** and ***John 8:1-11***

Ask for God's strength to continue your forgiveness for any person you are angry with.

CHAPTER TEN

RECOVERING FROM ANGER

Once if not more in our lives we have anger. It can be a temporary anger or it can be long-term anger that we have against someone or circumstances in our lives. We have even at times gotten angry with God.

There can be healthy anger and unhealthy anger. Healthy anger can be used for constructive reasons. Anger can be useful if it helps us to confront evil, right wrongs, or to change things for the good.

In *Ephesians 4:26* the Bible says, *"Be angry, and do not sin"*.

It is acceptable to have anger. It is a normal human emotion. There can be destructive anger that can actually cause us to sin. Destructive anger can cause us to hurt others, block our ability to love others, distort our thinking, and limit us to be able to think clearly. Destructive anger can also destroy us when we allow anger to consume our lives to the point of taking vengeance against another person. It can also cause us to be bitter, resentful, and full of hatred.

Anger can eat us alive. It consumes us. Anger is hard to rid yourself of without the use of anger management skills.

When we get angry we make a choice of how we react to that anger. We can use it constructively or destructively. The Bible says in:

Psalms 37:8 "Cease from anger, and forsake wrath. Do not fret-it only cause harm."

Anger causes us harm, spiritually and emotionally. The Bible is very clear on God's viewpoint of anger.

Proverbs 14:16 "A wise man fears and departs from evil, but a fool rages and is self-confident".

Proverbs 15:1 "A soft answer turns away wrath but a harsh word stirs up anger."

Proverbs 16:32 "He who is slow to anger is better than the mighty, and he who rules his spirit than he who takes a city."

We must learn how to control our anger to keep us from sinning. We all must make choices. We make a choice to either hold anger back or act out on it. When anger comes from a trauma in our life we must learn how to release the anger in a constructive way for spiritual healing.

The first lesson in anger management to rid yourself of anger is to learn what triggers your anger, how your body responds to anger, what physical manifestations of anger you adopt when enraged, and most importantly, the choice you make on how to act out on the anger.

How we express our anger is not something we are born with, it is how we learn or taught how we should express our anger. We learn how to express anger from our parent's styles. Children are influenced by the conflicts between their parents. Children are like sponges. The imitate everything they see. If they see their parents to act out violently by example then so will they. Parents can teach their children the best way to express their anger by teaching them. We are either taught as children to hold anger in or express it violently or calmly.

The two basic ways people tend to handle their angry feelings are by rage and resentment. These ways have very few benefits.

Rage is giving into our feelings of anger and blowing up   usually verbally.

Resentment is the act of holding anger back or holding feelings inside. Both of these can be harmful and sinful. We should never hold our anger in, but the emotions that are triggered from anger should be held back. The key to anger is in how we express it.

Being slow to anger is Scriptural and God knows we get angry, it is how we express it that can be damaging to our spirits and cause us to sin.

Anger can cause depression, guilt, un-forgiveness, and anxiety. For spiritual healing you have to release the anger you may have for someone. You again, have to forgive. Forgiveness is the key to control your anger.

Holding anger in will only build up further until you explode. Holding anger in can deeply affect your spirituality and your health. You should never hold your anger in.

Holding anger back is keeping yourself from expressing your anger immediately and violently. Holding anger back requires you to be able to keep from exploding, so to speak, and taking a step back to see things in perspective so that you can make a conscious and rational choice of how to express your anger.

I have listed some techniques to help you control your anger in the worksheet. These techniques will allow you to get in touch with your anger and learn to release it or control it.

Ephesians 4:26 "Be angry and do not sin."

God does not punish us for our anger. He understands we will have anger but He does give us direction in the Scriptures on how we should express our anger. He desires for us to learn how to have healthy anger. Learning how to use our anger constructively is our goal.

Anger can cause use to say things to someone we love that we really don't mean or to hurt someone we never intended to hurt. Once you have acted out on your anger and have expressed it by hurting others either, mentally or physically; it is often hard for the person you have hurt to forgive. It can often put up a wall between you and your loved ones that can affect your future relationship with them. Anger does not just affect you; it affects everyone around you.

Follow the techniques in the worksheet. These will help you to understand your anger, what triggers your anger, and how to control your anger. Practice these techniques on a daily basis. Each time you get angry and want to act on that anger, use these techniques step by step and follow through until the anger subsides. It will take time to learn how to use these steps but worth every minute you spend on them. Use these techniques to help you be able to be angry but not to sin.

Scripture Proverbs 29:11 "A fool vents his anger but a wise man holds them back."

Prayer: Dear Lord Jesus,

Help me Dear God, to hold my wrath and not sin. Lord give me the knowledge and wisdom to overcome my anger and release it to you. Teach me to overcome my anger and forgive those I am angry with and allow me to feel the peace of God in my spirit.

In Jesus' Precious Name,
Amen.

WORKSHEET

RECOVERING FROM ANGER

Be aware of your anger. Accept your anger and admit when you are angry.

Slow your anger down by counting to ten. Take deep breaths and try to relax your muscles.

If you are in a conflict with another person, separate your-self from the conflict or provoking situation. Ask the other person involved for postponement of the conversation, suggest another time and place for further discussion. Engage in calm self-talk or talk to a friend.

Control your thoughts. Anger begins as thoughts of self-pity, discouragement, or jealousy.

Identify the trigger for your anger. What caused you to become angry?

Mentally challenge irrational beliefs of expectations and acknowledge correct ones. In other words change your thought process. Is this a reason to get angry? What other perspective can I look at this situation?

Try not to be bothered by everything. Choose your battles.

Develop peace of mind.

Decide how or if it necessary to express anger.

Find alternative ways to express your anger.

EX: Keeping a diary, take a time-out, listening to music, or taking a walk.

CHAPTER ELEVEN

RECOVERING FROM ILLNESS

Illness, whether temporary or terminal of any type, can take a toll on your spirituality. Your faith level tends to diminish and depression sets in. Illness can affect every emotion you have.

Temporary illness may not affect us as greatly as terminal illness but can still take a toll on us.

Terminal patients can become angry with God, give up hope, become fearful, and feel forsaken by God. Any illness is hard to accept. Our first question is "Why me?" Why does God allow sickness? No one really knows the answer to that question. But sickness can be used to allow us to develop our faith, rely more on God, it can be used as a testimony to someone else that may be suffering from a similar illness or if healed as a testimony to God's power. It can be used to help us mature as children of God. It can be used to humble us. It can be used to allow us to help others.

God can also use our sickness to open our hearts to non-believers to develop a relationship with Him.

Illness can be used to actually save someone. Someone that may not have accepted Jesus may accept Him if found to have a terminal illness. Some people only turn to God when illness comes or some other crisis arises.

Only God knows the true answer to these questions. God does not desire for us to be afflicted with illness. Satan takes care of that. *John 10:10* states:

"The thief does not come except to steal, kill, and destroy. I have come that you may have life and have it more abundantly."

Satan is the giver of illnesses in our lives. He is the destroyer. God turns the bad things that Satan does to us for the good.

In *2 Corinthians 12:7-9* God took Paul's physical weakness and used it to glorify Himself. Paul wrote,

"A thorn in the flesh was given to me, a messenger of Satan to buffet me...I pleaded with the Lord three times that it might depart from me. And He said to me, "My grace is sufficient for you, for My Strength is made perfect in weakness".

Paul could gladly boast about his weakness so that Christ's power would rest on him.

"For when I am weak then I am strong."

2 Corinthians 12:10 "Therefore I take pleasure in my infirmities, in reproaches, in needs, in persecutions, in distresses, for Christ's sake. For when I am weak then I am strong."

Paul not only accepted his infirmities he took pleasure in them because he knew that God had given him grace and made his strength perfect in his weakness.

When you can't do it alone Christ is there to make you strong. We use our illnesses to help others like us to become strong. When they see our strength it will give them strength.

Does God heal us? Yes, in some instances. His Word says in

Isaiah 53:5, "But He was wounded for our transgressions, He was bruised for our iniquities. The chastisement for our peace was upon Him, and by His stripes we are healed.

1 Peter 2:24 "Who Himself bore our sins in his own body on the tree, that we, having died to sins, might live for righteousness-by whose stripes you were healed."

He desires for us to be healed. He can and He does heal.

I would like to share my own personal testimony with you about God's healing power in my life.

I had been under a tremendous amount of stress. This day was a particularly stressful day. I started having pain in my chest. The pain began to travel down my left arm and a heaviness set up in my chest. At that point, even though I was only 47 years old and I had never had a history of heart problems before, it came to me; I was having a heart attack.

I began to bow down and I cried out to God for His help. I pleaded with Him to keep me safe. I called my husband who is a minister and informed him of my pain. He was twenty minutes away and then we had to travel back into town for another twenty minutes. The pain grew in intensity. I was still crying and pleading with God to not allow anything bad to happen to me.

By the time we arrived at the hospital, the doctor informed me, I had already had 2 heart attacks and they told me that a third one would kill me. They began to sedate me to keep me from being in stress, started pumping me with blood thinners, inserted IV's, and began running tests on me.

The doctor saw on the echocardiogram that I had 2 lesions on my heart, there was a blockage, there was a leakage in my valves, and a portion of my heart was permanently damaged. They said they would have to do an emergency angioplasty and insert a stint. My sister said we need to pray over her and my husband led a prayer for healing and divine intervention.

While they had me in surgery, the doctor was looking for the blockage he had just seen on the echocardiogram but could not find it. The blockage was gone! Praise God! The doctor came out to speak to my family completely amazed and stated that he couldn't explain it but the blockage was gone and they didn't have to put the stint in after all.

When I had gone into surgery my family told me I was very pale but when I came out all the color had returned to my face. I was released from the hospital three days later.

While recovering from the heart attack, two weeks later I began to cry out in agony because of severe pain in my head. I had never felt pain in my head like that before. I called my husband who was again twenty minutes away at work. My son and my daughter-in-law were there with me. The pain was so severe I told my husband I could not wait for him to come and pick me up. My son was going to have to take me to the hospital. I again cried out to God to help me. I was in severe pain. My husband met me in the hospital along with the pastor and some of the church members and my family members.

The doctor asked me if I had headaches like this before and I told him no so he immediately put me under sedation and began taking MRI pictures. They discovered I was suffering from a brain aneurysm. They wanted to medi-flight me to Oklahoma City since we live in a small town and I needed to see specialists but we were having severe weather conditions so an ambulance took me.

As a team of doctors were deciding what needed to be done, my mom and sister came into my room and again my sister said let's pray over her and my husband and family gathered hands and agreed in prayer for my healing. My sister told the surgeons that God would be guiding their hands. They immediately took me in to do an angiogram and were prepared to drill into my head to put drainage tubes in. They weren't sure if I was going to make it.

My husband had to sign a lot of permission papers that were telling about the risks of the surgery and that I may not make it through it.

When they did the angiogram they discovered the bleeder was beginning to clot over. They said that this rarely happens. They said I could have a lot of brain damage and it could affect the limbs of my body, whether I would walk again, talk, or be paralyzed in any part of my body and they would just have to allow the brain to reabsorb the blood and see what happens. They put me in intensive care and by the third day I was rapidly improving. I had no brain damage, no muscle damage, or any damage at all. I had come out of it completely whole.

Praise you Jesus! He had done it again. The doctors could not believe how fast I had recovered. I was up walking on the fourth day and was almost back to my usual self. They kept me in the ICU saying that the aneurysms usually come in pairs and they wanted to do more tests to make sure there were no more bleeders. They ran test after test and they all came back normal. I was in the ICU for nine days.

I praise God every day for my healing. I give Him all of the glory and I tell anyone that will listen about how my God has saved my life.

God can and does heal! It is proven in my case. God brought me through. I praise Him every day for my life. God has given me an amazing testimony. I will continue to tell everyone I know or meet in the future. God uses what Satan puts on us to the good for His glory. Every doctor I still see still tells me how lucky I am that I have no paralysis of my limbs or damage to my body in any way. **It wasn't luck, IT WAS GOD!**

For those of you who may be going through trials of sickness, know that God Almighty can and will heal you. Keep your faith strong in Him. Have faith as a little child and lean on Him for complete healing. **He can and He will heal.** Maybe it won't be in the time we want but it will be in **His** time. He is using what Satan has come against you with for the good. He is working! God loves you and He desires to answer our prayers.

Mark 11:23 states, "For I say to whoever says unto this mountain, "Be thou removed and be cast into the sea," and does not doubt it in his heart but believes that those things He says will be done he will have whatever he says."

We will have whatever we say. Keep your faith strong.

Mark 11:24 "Therefore I say to you whatever things you ask when you pray, believe that you receive them and you shall have them."

Having faith in God for your healing will assist you in your spiritual healing. Allow the anger to go and rely on God's help. Pray until the answer comes. God desires to answer your prayers, **IN JESUS TIME**. But it will be the right time. You should receive your healing but if you don't then rejoice because God wants to use you in a tremendous way.

Scripture: Isaiah 53:5 "By His stripes we are healed".

Prayer: Oh Precious Father in Heaven.

Father I pray for your healing. Dear Lord I thank you for Your Word and Your Word does not return void. I thank you for the sacrifice you made for me Lord Jesus in giving up your life for me so that I may receive my divine healing. I thank you for my complete healing Lord and may it be in Your glory. Fill my spirit with Your precious Holy Spirit and draw me nearer to you. Use me Lord as a vessel for Your glory.

In Jesus' Precious Name,
Amen.

WORKSHEET

RECOVERING FROM ILLNESS

Pray to God for your healing and stand on the Word of God with your faith.

Have faith in God's healing for you.

Read ***2 Kings 20:1-11***

Remember healing will come in His time not ours. Stand firm.

Allow God to use your illness, your faith, and your strength to help others build their faith and strength.

Testify of your healing.

Don't give up and pray till the answer comes.

Get in solitude with God and allow Him to minister to you.

<u>BELIEVE, BELIEVE, BELIEVE</u>!!!

CHAPTER TWELVE

RECOVERY FROM DEPRESSION

Depression is an emotion that can affect you emotionally or physically. Clinical depression can be caused by a chemical imbalance in our bodies. We obviously can't discuss every form of depression, as there are many. If you are unsure of the reason for your depression the best thing to do would be to be evaluated by your physician to make sure your depression is not due to a chemical imbalance.

Emotional depression due to stress, whether it is always present or only present with the presence of stress, can be treated with medication also to ease the symptoms.

When we are depressed it is usually related to a specific life problem or a loss of something or someone. Women are more likely to suffer from depression than men. The risk factors in contributing to depression in women are as follows: living alone, sexual desirability, children, body chemistry, addiction to romantic love, marriage anger, fulfillment of motherhood, menopause, loneliness, shyness, or loss of a loved one, whether by death, abandonment, or rejection.

Depression can affect our bodies physically, such as insomnia, over sleeping, headaches, weight loss, weight gain, overeating, and mood swings.

Psalms 102: 1-2 provides a checklist of symptoms King David experienced during a stressful period in his life.

"Let my cry come to you, do not hide Your face from me in the day of my trouble;"

He was physically affected and lost meaning and purpose in his life.

"My days are consumed like smoke, and my bones are burned like a hearth. My heart is stricken and withered like grass." Psalms 102:1-2

Psalms 102:3-4 says he lost his appetite.

"I forgot to eat my bread"

He felt isolated and rejected.

Psalms 102:5-9 "I am like a pelican in the wilderness, I am like an owl in the desert. I lie awake." He cried, "I have eaten ashes like bread and mingled my drink with weeping".

Elijah had healthy and unhealthy depression. He did not eat, he was angry with God, he traveled alone, and he collapsed into sleep.

God encouraged Elijah to eat, drink, and rest. He brought him out of depression so Elijah would be able to listen to him.
Read the story of Elijah in *1 Kings 19:4-18.*

When we turn to our Lord Jesus Christ and look to Him for help, and encouragement He can cause our depression to subside. We have to keep in mind that our Heavenly Father is more powerful than our earthly father. We can turn to Him with any problem in our lives. He will always be there for us when we need to cry or talk. He is there to comfort us and lift us up. He desires for us to look to Him for comfort and protection.

Psalms 27 talks about how God is our light and salvation and our strength.

God wants to be our strength. He is the light we should look toward.

Psalms 34 discusses the happiness of those who trust in God.

He can and will deliver you from all your fears. He desires for us to be happy. Isn't it a comforting feeling to know that God can comfort, protect, and strengthen us? I get this vision in my head of being snuggled up in my bed at night all warm and cozy and God is right there holding me, comforting me, and protecting me.

Psalms 34:4 "I sought the Lord and He heard me and delivered me from all my fears".

Psalms 40 1-2 is about how faith will persevere in trial.

"I waited patiently on the Lord and He inclined to me, and heard me cry, He also brought me up out of a horrible pit, out of the miry day and set my feet upon a rock, and established my steps. He has put a new song in my mouth-Praise to our God."

God is there for us: day and night. He can bring us through the depths of depression into the joy of His Spirit.

Changing our thinking about things in our lives can ease our depression. Most of the time when we are depressed it is usually over things we cannot change. We must be ready to accept the things we cannot change and give those things and circumstances over to God. (See worksheet for techniques)

THE SERENITY PRAYER

God grant me the serenity

To accept the things I cannot change,

Courage to change the things I can,

And wisdom to know the difference.

The Serenity Prayer should be our motto in this life. The things we have no control over should be given to God. Accept the things we cannot change and the courage to change the things we can and the courage to know the difference. If we can use this in our everyday lives think of the stress that would be released from our shoulders.

God desires for His people to be healthy and happy. Read the story about Elijah in *1 Kings 19:4-18*. Allow this story to encourage you for your spiritual healing.

Use the worksheet at the end of this chapter for some techniques you can use to ease your depression symptoms. You can overcome depression. It may take some time. It definitely will not come overnight, but if you follow the techniques, this will help get you off to a good start.

I encourage you to pray and allow God to mend all that pains you. Allow Him to be your Heavenly Father and comfort you. Draw near to Him for encouragement. He will pull you through. Rely fully on God for comfort, strength, and protection. If God be for us then who can come against us?

Scripture: Isaiah 43:2-3 "When you pass through the waters, I will be with you; and through the rivers, they shall not overflow you. When you walk through the fire, you shall not be burned, nor shall the flame scorch you. For I am the Lord your God, The Holy One of Israel, your Savior."

Prayer: Dear Most Precious Heavenly Father,

How I long for you. I long for your presence in my life. Draw near to me Lord God for I long to be with you. Hear my prayer O God for healing. Release mew from this spirit of depression. Give me peace and joy in my spirit O God for I long to receive a renewed spirit.

Thank you for being my Heavenly Father for you are much wiser than any earthly father. Minister to my spirit with your Word. Thank you for complete healing in my life Dear God.

In Jesus' Name,
Amen.

WORKSHEET

RECOVERING FROM DEPRESSION

CHANGEABLES

Make a list of things that are causing problems in
your life that you can change.

_____
_____
_____
_____
_____
_____
_____
_____
_____
_____
_____
_____
_____
_____
_____
_____
_____
_____

UNCHANGEABLES

Make a list of things that are causing problems in your life that you have no control of changing.

_____

_____

_____

_____

_____

_____

_____

_____

_____

_____

Out of the list of changeables write down how you can change each item on the list and how you can solve it yourself. Take each one, one at a time, solve it if possible, and work down the list.

Out of the list of unchangeables pray to God and give Him this list to take care of. Don't try to change things yourself. Have the faith to allow God to work on this list. Give it over to Him and allow Him to change these unchangeables.

RECOVERING FROM DEPRESSION

Here are some techniques to use to help you with your depression symptoms. Read the list each day and follow the instructions.

Try to maintain a daily routine. Those who work should attempt to go to work every day. This will help prevent the depressed person from withdrawing and dwelling on negative thoughts.

If your work is in the home, attend to chores. Maintaining a daily routine will help you to keep a higher energy level. Continually lying in bed or on the sofa will gradually produce negative physical effects and promote sleeplessness at night.

Try to get out of the house, even for brief periods of time. This will help you to focus on others instead of yourself, and prevent negative thought patterns and rumination

Physical activity is very important for overcoming depression. Involvement in any type of physical activity can be very helpful. Studies have shown that increased levels of exercise and activity can actually lessen depressions that have been caused by biochemical imbalances.

If you can push yourself to do so, try to see family members and friends as much as possible, but only for brief periods of time.
Let your friends and family know that you need support, encouragement, and firmness.

Keep in mind that even severe depressions usually end.

Find someone with whom you can share your feelings and let them out.

If your appetite is poor, and you are losing weight, try to eat small amounts of food frequently. This will also help to maintain your energy level.

Strongly consider professional counseling.

Join a support group. (Christian if possible).

Talk to your pastor. If he is trained and has adequate time, he may be able to counsel with you. Otherwise, he may be able to refer you to a properly trained professional who can help. Your pastor will also lend his emotional support and encouragement as you work on the problem.

CHAPTER TWELVE

RECOVERING FROM FEAR, WORRY, AND ANXIETY

To receive spiritual healing we must have peace and joy in our spirits. We must be able to let go of the fear, worry, and anxiety that can create such havoc in our lives. Fear alone can cripple our lives but adding worry and anxiety on top of fear can disable your whole life and mind-set.

There are also anxiety disorders that require medication. Anxiety disorders are very prevalent in these last days. People in all walks of society have more stress now than ever before. Stress and anxiety can take a toll on not only our spiritual being but also our physical bodies. Stress can cause hypertension, can affect your blood pressure, and can cause strokes or heart attacks. Stress is what induced my heart attacks and aneurysm. How can we protect ourselves from stress? It is everywhere.

Let's discuss fear first. Fear is the emotion in our bodies that alerts us to danger. The experience of fear is very real. People also have fear of circumstances that are perceived. Fear of something that has not or may not happen can completely take over our thinking. It prevents us from thinking rationally. When in fear of perceived circumstances the question of "What if" is never ending in our minds. When we fear perceived circumstances such as dying, losing a child, spouse, or job, or losing our health it keeps us from living a full, happy life. The fear itself takes over every aspect of our lives. We allow the fear to take over our mind-set.

Now with fear comes worry. Fear and worry are not the same. Fear is a reaction to danger, worry is not an emotion but activity that produces anxiety. When we worry, we are usually worrying about things that have not happened yet: or has happened and we dwell on it constantly. Worry can also produce stress in our lives that affect our health.

When we worry it is usually over things that we have no control of. We don't turn it over to God or pray about it, we instead worry and we try to think of ways that we can fix it ourselves.

Now let's talk about anxiety. Anxiety keeps a person from relaxing. It is an inner feeling of unrest, nervousness, and uneasiness. It produces rapid heartbeat, dry mouth, increased blood pressure, faintness, or dizziness. It affects our body much more than worry or fear.

There are several anxiety disorders, such as, generalized anxiety disorder, which is chronic tension in many different situations, phobias, which is fear that may be associated with an object, place or event, obsessive compulsive disorder, which is fear hidden behind a variety of obsessive compulsions such as ritual hand washing, etc.

Post Traumatic Stress Disorder is an anxiety disorder associated with a traumatic event in our lives.

Panic attacks are the sudden onset of overwhelming anxiety being paralyzed by the fight or flight response. These forms of anxiety can be controlled with medication. See your physician if you suspect you may have any of the above-mentioned disorders.

God does not hold anxiety against us. Some Scripture condemns a certain form of anxiety. In *John 14:1* Jesus said,

"Let not your heart be troubled."

He is talking about worry. Worry cannot solve our problems. Read *Matthew 6:25-34* about the Sermon on the Mount. He talks about how destructive anxiety can be. When we stop worrying, the anxiety will stop, when the anxiety stops, the fear will desist.

In *2 Timothy 1:7* it says,

"For God has not given us a spirit of fear but of power and of love, and of a sound mind."

He hasn't given us a spirit of fear. He gives us power through His Name. Fear is a waning of faith. When we fear we are not fully relying on God for His protection.

God wants us to have a healthy, sound mind. *Hebrews 13:5* says,

"Let your conduct be without covetousness; be content with such things as you have. For He Himself has said, "I will never leave you nor forsake you".

He will never leave us or forsake us. He is omnipresent. His present will constantly remain in our lives.

Hebrews 13:6, on fear, says,
"The Lord is my helper; I will not fear, What can man do to me?"

We should not fear when we have someone as huge and powerful as God on our side, the Alpha and Omega, the beginning and the end, the Omnipresent.

1 Peter 5 says, *"Casting all your care upon Him for He cares for you".*

We can always depend on God. Let Him do the worrying for you. Cast all your care upon Him.

Release the fear and allow yourself to feel the protection of His mighty hands.

Go to the worksheet and I will give you some techniques on healthier patterns you can adopt. Allow yourself to experience the peace that comes in God. Give it all to Jesus. Count on His love and His Word! Count on Him!!

Scripture: Deuteronomy 31:8   "And the Lord, He is the One who goes before you, He will not leave you nor forsake you; do not fear, nor be dismayed".

Prayer: Dear God,

Allow me to be able to give it all to You Father. I want You to take all my worries and cares away. Father I put my worries in Your Hands and I know You will take care of it for me. I trust in Your Word and Your Promises. Help me to be a person of faith and allow you to do Your Work in me. I thank You and I worship You. I adore You.

In Jesus' Name,
Amen

WORKSHEET

RECOVERING FROM FEAR, WORRY, AND ANXIETY

Read *Deuteronomy 31*:6

Turn to God first. Read *1 Peter 5:7.*

Focus on the solution, not the problem. Read *Matthew 14:22-2*

Stop wasting energy on worrying. Read *Matthew 6:25-34.*

Keep your thoughts on God in order to have peace. Read *Isaiah 26:3*

Pray. Read *Philippians 4:4-9.*

Direct your attention toward your true source of hope. Read *Psalms 91:2.*

Make a list of things you have control of and can change and your plan for changing them.

_____

_____

_____

_____

_____

_____

Make a list of things you cannot change and that you are now turning over to God.

_____

_____

_____

_____

_____

_____

CHAPTER FOURTEEN

RECOVERING FROM GUILT AND SHAME

We all experience guilt and shame some time in our lives. We may feel guilt over not being a perfect parent, failing to fulfill a promise or many other reasons.

We all fall short of being perfect. No one is perfect. The only perfect human being was Jesus.

People handle guilt basically the same with the exception of those that dwell on their guilt. Some people may have guilt for no special reason. These few people handle guilt totally different.

There is a difference between feeling guilty and being guilty. If someone breaks a law then obviously they are guilty, whether they feel they are or not, but there are those that feel guilt just because they feel they have fallen short of another's expectations of them. They feel guilt to the extreme even though they are not guilty of anything. They are still nagged by these feelings. They feel that if they fail to be perfect then they are somehow guilty of something. They may not know why the feel guilty, but the emotion is still there, very strongly! It weighs on their minds and they feel like they have to right whatever they feel they did wrong.

God knows we are not perfect and we may sometimes fall short of His expectations, but we have to allow ourselves to be imperfect without feeling guilty about it. God says in His Word in:

Romans 8:1 "There is therefore now no condemnation to those who are in Christ Jesus."

God does not want guilt to be allowed in the sanctified life where there is no basis for the guilt. Satan is the one who puts the spirit of guilt upon us. Satan is known as "the accuser" in **Revelations 12:10.**

In our minds we all have what is known as the mental record player. The mental record player plays over and over in our minds that which we cannot let go. Satan will cause that mental record player in our minds to play over and over again to hold us in bondage. This can prevent our spiritual healing. Satan's work is to create condemnation in our spirits, to keep us bound in him.

The Holy Spirit's work results in conviction, forgiveness, and restoration. When guilt feelings occur we must stand on the Word.

Romans 8:1, "There is therefore now no condemnation to those who are in Christ Jesus."

We must break the mental record that keeps repeating in our minds.

Most people know when they are guilty and in those cases they simply ask for forgiveness and can move on but for those who cannot, are filled with overwhelming hopelessness and guilt. God forgives you when you ask for forgiveness and he remembers it no more.

Hebrews 8:12 "For I will be merciful to their unrighteousness and their sins and their lawless deeds, and I will remember them no more."

You need to find forgiveness with yourselves. Ask God's forgiveness, accept His cleansing love, correct the misdeed, if appropriate, and forget it. Permanent relief from moral guilt comes from God's forgiveness. Turn off the mental record player and ask God for the strength to do this.

2 Corinthians 7:10 "For Godly sorrow produces repentance leading to salvation, not to be regretted, but the sorrow the world produces is death."

God doesn't want to condemn us. He wants us to live free from condemnation.

Jeremiah 33:8 "I will cleanse them of all their iniquity by which they have sinned and by which they have transgressed against me."

Romans 3:23-24, "For all have sinned and fallen short of the glory of God, being justified freely by His grace through the redemption that is in Jesus Christ."

We have all fallen short. There is no one perfect. Allow yourselves to be only human, and forgive yourself freely and dwell on the Word of God that He sanctifies you. Now you have to allow yourself to be sanctified. Release the hold of bondage Satan has on you to be able to no longer condemn yourself.

Hebrews 10:2 "For the worshippers once purified, would have no more consciousness of sins."

Once we have been purified He wants us to have no more consciousness of sins. Not that when we sin we should not ask for forgiveness, but once the Father has forgiven us we are to remember it no more just as He has. We are to accept the forgiveness provided to us. Don't allow Satan to cause you to feel a continual guilt. He remembers it no more so should we.

Accept yourself as an imperfect child of God, accept His forgiveness, and forgive yourself. Reach for the inner peace only God can provide and free yourself from the bondage of Satan's lies.

Strive for your spiritual healing by receiving your forgiveness from God, forgiving yourself, and accept the peace that God desires for you.

Scripture: Hebrews 10:22 "Let us draw near with a true heart in full assurance of faith, having our hearts sprinkled from an evil conscience and our bodies washed with pure water."

Prayer: Father I thank you for Your forgiveness and Your love. I accept Your forgiveness and I now will forgive myself. I understand that I am unable to always be perfect and all I can expect is to strive for the qualities of Jesus. Father I now release the spirit of unforgiveness of myself and allow Your forgiveness to free me of guilt and shame. I no longer have to condemn myself and live in guilt. Thank you Jesus for Your free gift of forgiveness. No longer will I allow Satan to keep me in bondage. I praise and adore You.

In Jesus' Name,
Amen.

WORKSHEET

RECOVERING FROM GUILT AND SHAME

Pay attention to guilt feelings.

Determine if the guilt is a result of realistic or unrealistic expectations.

Remember you are only human.

If guilt feelings are a result of sin ask God's forgiveness and accept His forgiveness.

Forgive yourself.

Determine if guilt feelings are unrealistic or unpurposeful.

Turn off the mental record player that repeats in your mind. This will take a lot of practice.

Read **_Psalms 32, Psalms 38, Psalms 51,_** and **_Psalms 89._**

CHAPTER FIFTEEN

RECOVERING FROM BITTERNESS

What is bitterness? Bitterness is a nagging feeling of rage, anger, and sometimes hate. We may be bitter from a tragedy that has happened in our lives, a person we feel may have done us wrong, or at God.

God allows everything in our lives to happen. He doesn't like it when we have to go through trials. He will use what Satan puts upon us for the good. He uses it sometimes to test our faith, He may use it to test our strength, or He may use it just to see if we need Him. He and only He knows what we need in our lives to grow up spiritually, to gain strength, and build our faith.

First we will discuss bitterness with tragedy. A tragedy could be an accident that has affected our bodies medically or emotionally. When tragedy happens who is the first person we blame? God.

In the book of Job, God allowed Satan to attack Job. He attacked his livestock, killed his children, gave him painful boils from his head to his toes, and he still never blamed God or sinned because of it. God allows believers to go through testing with trials. It allows us to draw nearer to Him; it tests our strength, strengthens our faith, makes us depend on God more, and matures us as Christians.

When we go through trials we do one of two things; we either pray more to God for relief or we blame God and become bitter.

God screens the trials in our lives allowing only those that accomplish His plan.

He wants to rescue us from our sin. He doesn't like to see us suffer or be in pain but it is a requirement for our calling.
God Himself suffered when He allowed Jesus to die on the cross for us. Jesus suffered by having to die on the cross.

Proverbs 14:10 says*, **"But the heart knows its own bitterness, and a stranger does not share its joy."***

Bitterness towards someone who has hurt us is the most common bitterness. This world is so full of evil that our children are being abused and killed, rapes, murders, and broken families. When we have bitterness for others it does not hurt the person we are bitter with it only hurts us. It can consume us on a daily basis with anger and rage. We dwell on it on a daily basis. It can rob us of our health; our spirit; our relationship with others; our relationship with God; and finally our salvation. It drains us emotionally. What does it do to the person we are bitter with? Absolutely nothing! So whom does bitterness hurt? US!

How can we heal our hearts of bitterness: through the contentment of God's love? It is very hard to let go of bitterness but it is definitely worth it for peace in our spirits.

2Corinthians 6:10 says, *"As sorrowful, yet always rejoicing."*

We have to put God first on our list. We have to pursue God. When we are bitter it takes our focus off of God. It affects our relationship with Him.

We have to overcome bitterness by overcoming with God. We have to forgive the person or tragedy we are bitter with. We must understand the lesson God is trying to show us when we are bitter with God.

Forgiveness is the only true remedy for bitterness. It will take time; it is a process.

Remember the chapter that discussed the imagination wins over the will? We have to add forgiveness to our imaginations.

Bitterness is a poison and will eat at our spirits until there is nothing left.

Acts 8:23 "For I see that you are poisoned by bitterness and bound by iniquity."

Ephesians 4:26 "Be angry and do not sin. Do not let the sun go down on your wrath."

Ephesians 4:31-32 "Let all bitterness, wrath, anger, clamor, and evil speaking be put away from you with all malice. And be kind to one another, tenderhearted, forgiving one another, even as Christ forgave you."

Until you are ready to forgive and allow the bitterness to leave, you will always have a troubled heart and it will hinder your spiritual healing. Pray and allow God to take away the hurt, the anger, the rage, and the bitterness. Once the forgiveness begins the bitterness will subside; and you will have the true peace and healing God intended for you.

Scripture: James 3:14 "But if you have bitter envy and self seeking in your hearts, do not boast and lie against the truth."

Prayer: Father in Heaven,

I pray you will take this bitterness from my heart. Help me to be forgiving of others that have harmed me in the past. Give me a forgiving heart and a peace within my spirit. I am giving my bitterness to you and pray for your forgiveness. Thank you for your undying love and peace.

In Jesus' Name
Amen.

WORKSHEET

RECOVERING FROM BITTERNESS

Recognize your bitterness.

Determine who or what you are bitter with and write it down.

Make a list of reason you are bitter.

Take the list and pray over it asking God to forgive you. Ask God to allow you to forgive the situation or person you are angry or bitter with. Ask God to remove the bitterness from your heart. Do this on a daily basis until the bitterness is gone.

 If this bitterness ever returns repeat the exercise again.

Put forgiveness for this person or situation in the imagination by repeating this:

 I forgive _____ and I am no longer bitter with
                    Name of person
  you.

The imagination will usually win over the will. Do this exercise numerous times throughout the day.

CHAPTER SIXTEEN

RECOVERING FROM LOW SELF-WORTH

How you value yourself is how you value God. If your value in yourself is low then you don't have much value for God.

God has much value for you. He loves you as much His own child: Jesus Christ.

You may be thinking, "How can God love me?" I am so unworthy. God knows our imperfections but yet He still treasures us.

Jeremiah 1:5 "Before I formed you in the womb, I knew you; before you were born, I sanctified you".

Before we were born He loved us and knew the plan He had for us. He had already sanctified us. God does the same for everyone.

Psalms 139:16 "Your eyes saw my substance, being yet unformed. And in Your book they all were written. The days fashioned for me. When as yet there were none of them."

He gave each of us our own personalities and gave each of our own purpose, **<u>before</u>** we were born.

Low self-esteem can greatly affect our spiritual health. It hinders everything God has planned for us. Someone with low self-esteem prohibits them from answering God's calling for them and can hinder the blessings God has for us.

Psalms 8:3-6 "When I consider Your heavens the work of Your fingers, the moon and the stars, which You have ordained. What is man that You are mindful of him, and the Son of Man that You visit Him?"
For You have made him a little lower than the angels, and You have crowned Him with glory and honor.
You have made him to have dominion over the works of Your hands."

God laid tremendous responsibility on us. He had faith in us and gave us dominion over all that He made. If He can have that kind of faith in us then why is it so hard for us to have faith in ourselves and in God?

Low self-esteem generally describes feelings of self-hate, rejection, and an ability to accept oneself as special and unique. We are to never be vain and to always be humble but to never demean ourselves or think lowly of ourselves.

Paul encourages us to think soberly of ourselves.

"For I say through grace given to me to everyone who is among not to think of himself more highly than he ought (meaning to humble yourselves) *but to think soberly as God has dealt to each on a measure of faith." Romans 12:3*

We are not to be vain but we are not to hate ourselves either. When we look and evaluate ourselves honestly and by understanding our value to God then we can have a healthy self-esteem.

We must value ourselves as God values us.

Romans 12:3 gives us insight on the consequences of a distortion of self-image.

We have to first be honest with how we feel about ourselves. This is an important step for spiritual healing. We have to admit our weaknesses cherish and our strengths.

Galatians 2:20 says, *"I have been crucified with Christ; It is no longer I who live, but Christ who lives in me, and the life which I now live in the flesh I live by faith in the Son of God who loved me and gave Himself for me."*

God would never have sacrificed His Son for people He didn't love and cherish. He had to have loved us to sacrifice His own child. He values us tremendously.

Christ *lives in us*. This alone should cause us to see our value in Him. That should make us feel very special to be chosen as a temple for Him. It is no longer we who live but Christ who lives in us.

Galatians 3:26 says, *"For you are all sons of God through faith in Jesus Christ."*

Galatians 4:7 "Therefore you are no longer a slave but a sons and if a son, then as heir of God through Christ."

How can we feel low of ourselves with Christ living in us? Are we perfect? No, no one is perfect but God has accepted our imperfections.

Ephesians 2:4 "But God who is rich in mercy, because of His great love for us".

He has GREAT love for us! How can we degrade ourselves?

When we devalue ourselves we devalue God because He lives in us.

Stand on the Word of God, and realize your value in Him and then realize your value in yourself.

God's love is so infallible and without boundaries. He made you and knew you in the womb. You are a special person and so unique, unlike any other. He gave us each our own personalities. He knows the number of hairs on our head. We are made uniquely, unlike any other. He has so much value for us. Let's start today to find the value we should have in ourselves. We are made perfect in Him.

Scripture: 1 Peter 2:9-10 *"But you are a chosen generation, a royal priesthood, a holy nation, His own special people, that you may proclaim the praises of Him who called you out of darkness into His marvelous light, who once were not a people but are now the people of God, who had not obtained mercy, but now have obtained mercy."*

Prayer: Dear Father,

I thank you for choosing me to be in your royal priesthood. Thank your for accepting me for who and what I am. I will now value myself as I value You. I see myself as a child of God, imperfect but made righteous by your mercy. Thank you for loving me. I love you as I love myself.

In Jesus' Name,
Amen.

WORKSHEET

RECOVERING FROM LOW SELF-ESTEEM

Do not criticize or degrade yourself. This will undermine your confidence and self-acceptance.

Use positive reinforcement. Value your positive points and accept them as God's gift.

Learn to value your true worth. Celebrate your good points and ask God for help with your weak points. Realize your value in God and celebrate it.

Value others. Valuing others will help you to value yourself.

Make a list of all those who love you and be honest with yourself.

Make a list of all of your good points.

Take the list of your good points and read them each day until you start to believe it. This will take some time but eventually you will start to see your value in Christ.

CHAPTER SEVENTEEN

RECOVERING FROM GRIEF AND LOSS

What is grief? Grief is defined as an intense emotion or deep sadness over a loss. It doesn't matter if the loss is a family member, friend, job, or pet. It doesn't matter if the loss is by a death, abandonment, or rejection. A loss is a loss. To deny your grief over the loss is very damaging to emotional, physical, and spiritual health. Refusing to accept the grief by hiding it or suppressing your emotions is damaging and can prolong the grief and affect the rest of your life tremendously.

Dealing with loss is the only way your life can move forward in a normal way. "Mourning" is the expression of grief. People mourn and handle grief in many different ways.

Grief is very painful and can be hard to face. It can take 1-3 years to accept the loss and mourn. It is very frightening to have to face the loss and gain perspective on the affect it has on the rest of your life.

Emotions associated with grief are sadness, fear, angriness, bitterness, guilt, numbness, helplessness, hopelessness, emptiness, and loneliness.

Grief is a process that must be processed through our minds. We have to learn how to express grief. People don't like to talk about their grief and often try to keep it hidden.

There are four stages of grief. These stages are not in any one order but can come in any order.

Denial is the first stage. When people experience loss they don't want to acknowledge it. They feel numb and don't want to accept the loss.

The second stage is releasing their emotions. This is usually by anger with people and God. They don't understand the reason for the loss and often ask, "Why?" Some may release their emotions through tears. Others may release their anger in destructive ways.

The third stage is feelings of anger and guilt. They blame themselves for the loss. They feel lost and are unable to know how to get past it and move on. They often suffer from depression.

The fourth state involves acceptance of the loss. They have to reorganize their lives and fit back in to people's lives. They may have a new role in their lives to fill.

We have to learn how to feel and express pain in more healthy ways without denial and avoidance. It is perfectly normal and acceptable to express your grief through tears, solitude, and with anger. Holding in your grief will not allow you to accept the loss and move on. Grief must be expressed.

Grieving people will need a great deal of support from friends and family. Helping the grieving person to express and deal with their emotions will help the person to reconnect.

Isaiah 53:3-5 it states, *"He was despised and rejected, a Man of sorrows and acquainted with grief. He was wounded for our transgressions and bruised for our iniquities; the chastisement for our peace was upon Him."*

Even Jesus suffered great loss and grief. He can help you through any losses and grief that we may suffer through in our lives. God made it so that Jesus had to feel grief so He would be familiar how we feel so He could comfort us. Grief can overcome us so drastically that it may require us to seek counseling. This is acceptable also. Those who may have trouble expressing or accepting their loss may need to seek the advice of a professional. This is nothing to be ashamed about. Losses can have great affect on us.

The grieving process is by no means easy, but it is necessary for complete spiritual healing. All of the earthly baggage that we carry with us in this life affects our spiritual health. We need to have the skills that are necessary for spiritual peace. When we give all of our baggage to God and allow Him to work then and only then will His divine plan for us in our lives take place to allow us to have divine peace and spiritual health He intends for us.

Ecclesiastes 3:4 "A time to weep and a time to laugh, a time to mourn, and a time to dance."

There is a time and a season for everything in our lives. When someone passes others are born. This is a part of life we have to confront and accept. We should never be afraid of expressing our grief. Expressing our grief doesn't mean we are letting go of our loved one, it just means we are coming into an acceptance of the loss. We then will have our memories of the loss to always comfort us.

Grief can hold us captive and rob us of our joy in the Lord. There is a time to cry and a time to laugh. To get to the time to laugh we have to allow the grief process to take place. When loss occurs we often think that this is the end of the world. Will it change our lives? Yes! Can we make it through this change? Yes! Should we allow our lives to completely stop by our grieving because of the loss? No! Those that suffer grief are afraid of continuing their pattern of living because they don't want to feel that they are forgetting the person they have lost. They feel guilty if they try to continue to live their life. They feel guilty that they are still alive and their loved one has passed. You should never feel guilty because of a loved one passing on before you. Look ahead and know that you will see them again. Fill your life with the thought of knowing they are waiting on you.

John 14:1 *"Let not your heart be troubled, you believe in God, believe also in Me."*

Jesus doesn't desire us to be troubled. He desires for us to be joyful in the Lord and full of peace, but when we are troubled He is there to carry us through.

Allow your grief to go through its process. It is difficult for anyone to suffer loss. We have to be able to process grief in a healthy way to keep our spiritual health in tact. Allow God to console you and to assist you in your grief. God will carry your through to make it as easy as possible for you. Spend time with God in prayer and He can give you insight on your loss. Express your grief in a healthy way. Allow yourself to live again. God will pull you through. Allow for His comfort and understanding.

Set your sights on Him.

Scripture 1 Thessalonians 4:13-14 "But I do not want you to be ignorant, brethren, concerning those who have fallen asleep, lest you sorrow as others who have no hope. For if we believe that Jesus died and rose again, even so God will bring Him those who sleep in Jesus."

Prayer: Father in Heaven,

You know my grief. You know my sorrow and suffering of my loss. Father I give it all up to you. Help me through my pain and allow me to grieve and heal. Lord be with me in my loneliness and comfort me in my loss. I thank you for being with me in difficult times. I give it all to you for my complete healing. I love and worship you.

In Jesus' Name,
Amen.

WORKSHEET

RECOVERING FROM GRIEF AND LOSS

STAGES OF GRIEF

Denial- learn how to feel and express the pain more truly without the denial and avoidance. Accept the loss.

Release your emotions- The sooner you can experience the release of your emotions the sooner the grieving process will end. It is all right to cry and express your emotions.

Feeling of guilt and anger- Do not hold yourself hostage with guilt. It is okay to feel anger in a healthy way.

Acceptance of loss- Accepting the loss will allow you to grieve the loss, which is a necessary process for renewal. Reorganize you life, filling new roles, and reconnecting with those around you are all healthy and important facets of the healing process.

CHAPTER EIGHTEEN

EMOTIONAL WELL-BEING

How can we even think of healthy emotional well-being with the society we live in? With all the happenings in this world, it is taking a toll on our emotional and spiritual health in our society. You can't turn on the television or radio, or pick up a newspaper without hearing all of the disturbing events. How does a person keep their sanity? It has an affect on everyone.

How we look at situations definitely takes a toll on us. Our outlook can be positive or negative. Only we have the power to control how it affects us.

We have to learn how we can look at all of these evil situations and how we allow it to affect our lives.

In *2 Timothy 1:7* we discussed previously how God desires His people to have a sound mind, peace and joy. To have any of those we have to believe in God's Word, which requires faith.

Healthy faith can help us keep our self-worth in tact. Our self-worth is very important for emotional well-being. Without a healthy self-worth we cannot have spiritual health.

Those with low self-worth have a difficult time accepting forgiveness from God. They don't think they are worth God's forgiveness. Even with forgiveness from God, they still cannot gain peace and joy, due to the fact that they don't forgive themselves or continually live with guilt.

God deems each and every one of us valuable, changeable, loveable, and forgivable. We have to allow ourselves to accept His value in us. We have to value ourselves, love ourselves, and most importantly, forgive ourselves. This is the first step in emotional health.

Faith allows us to understand why we go through trials in our lives. It helps us to understand that without trial comes immaturity. We can't grow spiritually without trials. Trials make us more knowledgeable, and stronger. It prepares us for many trials we have to face in this imperfect world.

Faith moderates our stress and tension. With faith we understand and believe that God is carrying us through. Faith allows us to see God as our Heavenly Father and that He loves us.

Our faith can eliminate any anger we may have. We can manage anger better with faith. With faith we can turn bitter anger into constructive anger.

How do we gain emotional health? We pray through to the Father above. In the worksheet are some things you can do to gain or maintain emotional health.

God can give us our emotional health by helping us to build our faith.

Joshua 1:5-9 "No Man shall be able to stand before you all the days of your life; as I was with Moses, so shall I be with you. I will never leave you nor forsake you. Be strong and of_good courage, for to this people you shall divide as an inheritance the land, which I swore to their fathers to give them. Only be strong and very courageous, that you may observe to do according to all the law, which my servants commanded you; do not turn from it to the right hand or the left; that you may prosper wherever you go. This Book of the Law shall not depart from your mouth, but you shall meditate in it day and night, that you may observe to do according to all that is written in it. For then you will make your way prosperous, and then you will have good success. Have I not commanded your? Be strong and of good courage; do not be afraid nor be dismayed, for the Lord your God is with you wherever you go."

God talks about how much He loves us. He will never leave us nor forsake us, and He has made us part of Jesus' inheritance. He wants us to be strong and courageous, never waning to the left or the right. He will always be with us. We are to meditate on the Word day and night so we can be prosperous. We are never to be dismayed or afraid for He is with us always.

Psalms 4:7 "You have put gladness in my heart".

Proverbs 14:30 "A sound heart is life to the body, but envy is rottenness to the bones."

John 16:20 "Most assuredly, I say to you that you will weep and lament, but the world will rejoice; and you will be sorrowful, but your sorrow will be turned into joy."

He promises that we may weep and lament but He will turn our sorrow into joy. He will restore us.

Philippians 4:9 "The things, which you learned and received and heard, and saw in me, these do, and the God of Peace will be with you."

The things in which we have learned in His Word we are to receive and do. He gives us instruction through His Word. For each and every trial we go through we can find the answer to in the Scriptures.

Faith gives us the emotional support to keep our spiritual health and emotional well-being in tact.

God provides for us in every way. Our faith will get us through any emotional storm. Building healthy faith is vital for spiritual health. We have

Scripture after Scripture of God's undying love for us. He provides us a way through every thing we go through in this life. He allows the Word to provide a shelter and a safe haven for us to go to. He provides the Word for our renewing of our spirits. We only have to accept the wonderful gifts that He has provided for us. If we turn to the Word and to God for each trial we go through we will always come out stronger than we went in.

Use the worksheet for steps to building your emotional health. Stand on God's promises to reclaim victory for peace and joy in your life. Claim what is rightfully yours. Everything is this world has a price on it but the Word of God is free. We can have the keys to a true healthy, joyful, and peaceful life. God has provided the answers for us. Take your rightful place in God's eyes. The gift is free.

Scripture: Colossians 3:12-17 "Therefore as the elect of God, holy and beloved, put on tender mercies, kindness, humility, meekness, longsuffering, bearing with one another, and forgiving one another, if anyone has a complaint against another; even as Christ forgave you, so also must you do. But above all these things put on love, which is the bond of perfection. And let the peace of God rule in your hearts, to which also you were called in one body; and be thankful. Let the Word of God dwell in you richly in all wisdom, teaching admonishing one another in psalms, and hymns and spiritual songs, singing with grace in your hearts to the Lord. And whatever you do in word and deed, do all in the name of the name of the Lord Jesus, giving thanks to God the Father through Him."

Prayer: Father,

Help me to live my life according to Your Word for my spiritual health.

Guide me to obedience and help me to forgive and be the elect of God. Thank you for Your Word as a guide for my life. Continue to be with me, molding me for your divine plan.

In Jesus' Name,
Amen.

WORKSHEET

EMOTIONAL HEALTH

GAINING EMOTIONAL HEALTH

Relief does not come overnight. It may take weeks or months. Repeat this process till relief comes.

Do not internalize pain.
Be honest with God about your emotional pain.

While in prayer with God allow your emotions to flow- anger, pain, tears, and fear.

Ask God to give you a new outlook on how to feel or think.

Thank and praise God for your new way of thinking.

Repeat this process as needed for complete healing.

Read and stand on *Lamentations 3:22-23.*
"Through the Lord's mercies we are not consumed, because His compassions fail not."

They are new every morning; Great is your Faithfulness.”

Claim your freedom and new insight. Take victory in your hands. Your victory comes through faith. Your emotional healing is around the corner! Praise God for it!

CHAPTER NINETEEN

RESTORATION

Psalms 51:10 "Create in me a clean heart, O God, and renew a steadfast spirit within me".

Being restored in Christ is when we give it all to God. We repent our sins, turn from it, accept responsibility, face the truth, regain power from God, and walk in the light of God's righteousness with you.

There can be restoration from sin and there can be restoration to a renewed spirit. Spiritual sickness can greatly affect our divine relationship with God. To be restored is to be carried back into the arms of Jesus.

To be restored we have to allow complete humility in our spirits. We open our spirit to a renewing of our minds.

We humble ourselves to the depth of our souls. We accept our sins, admit, them, ask for His forgiveness, and forgive ourselves. We accept His forgiveness and His healing.

Job 33:26 "He shall pray to God, and He will delight in Him, He shall see His face with joy. For He restores to man his righteousness."

He restores man in His righteousness. Righteousness is freely given. We don't have to work toward righteousness.

This is something that only God can give us. God can restore our spirit to righteousness.

Psalms 23:3 "He restores my soul; He leads me in the paths of righteousness."

Spiritual healing can only come through God by faith in His promises. He can and will restore us to righteousness.

We are forgiven when we ask God to intervene in our lives.

Psalms 51 says *"Restore to me the joy of Your salvation and uphold me by Your generous spirit."*

All we need to do is ask for restoration of our spirits for complete healing and to restore us to be used by Him for His glory and to give it all to Jesus. When we humble ourselves to His Word He will mold us into mature Christians. Allow Him to mold us into what He wants us to be, not what we would like ourselves to be. Make room for Him in your spirit. We allow Him to restore us to our salvation.

Jeremiah 30:17 "For I will restore health to you and heal you of your wounds".

This verse is not just talking about our physical wounds but also our emotional and spiritual wounds. We can never be used by God, without our spiritual health. He will restore our spiritual and physical health to us. He can take all the baggage we have been carrying up to this point and carry it for us. He will restore our spiritual health.

We have to be spiritually healthy ourselves before we can ever be a candle for others. We have to be a light to others as well as to God. He gives us this light through His Holy Spirit. God works through us by way of the Holy Spirit. This is why

We should seek to be baptized in the Holy Spirit. Our bodies are the Temple for the Holy Spirit. The Holy Spirit cannot inhabit us if the candle is burned out. Our spirituality has to be healthy to be productive.

Zechariah 9:12 "Return to the stronghold Your prisoners of hope. Even today I declare that I will restore double to you."

What is the stronghold? **The Word of God.** We have to return to the Word of God, to Him, for restoration that is doubled to you. We will be restored in double quantities. He will double our restoration. Without the stronghold of the Word of God we would have to carry the baggage of this dirty, evil world. God desires to restore our spiritual health.

Praise God! We serve a mighty and loving God who will never leave us nor forsake us. A God who will be there in our time of need, day or night; no matter what day of the week. He is ever present in our lives waiting to grant us the restoration and the salvation that Jesus has earned for us by dying on the cross. Why would we ever want Jesus' death to be in vain? Accept His complete restoration and allow Him to inhabit your spirit through the rest of your life. Who would want to give up the many gifts He has promised us? Who would ever want to make it through another day without the peace, joy, and victory we have in Christ Jesus?

Not me!!!!!

Not you!!!!!!!

Thank you Jesus! Praise your Holy Name.

Scripture: Acts 3:20-21 "And that He may send Jesus Christ, who was preached to you before, whom Heaven must receive until the times of restoration of all things, which God has spoken by the mouth of all His prophets since the world began".

Prayer: Dear Most Heavenly Father,

Thank you for the restoration of my spirit. I want to be everything you want me to be. Do your work in me so that I may fulfill Your divine plan that You have for me. Bless me in all that I do and thank you for my spiritual healing. I praise you and I thank you.

In Jesus' Name,
Amen.

WORKSHEET

RESTORATION

Ask for God's forgiveness being very honest with yourself.

Ask for restoration for your spirit. Get alone with God and express your emotions freely while in prayer.

Accept His gift of healing.

Testify to someone this week about your restoration.

Lead someone else to his or her restoration.

Spend time in prayer every day. Make yourself a prayer journal and keep track of how much time you spend in fellowship with God.

Spend time in the Word every day. Make a Bible journal. Write down the passages you read each day. You should be able to read through the whole Bible in one year. Strive for this goal.

Read ***Colossians 3:12-17.***

CHAPTER TWENTY

SALVATION

I cannot in good conscience close this book without touching on the subject of salvation. God desires all of His children to be lifted up with Jesus into the Heavens upon His return.

Salvation is to be saved, accepting Jesus Christ as your Lord and Savior, believing that He came to save you and that He died on the cross for your sins.

We will never earn our worthiness to be included in the family of God had it not been through God's grace. He freely gives us His mercy and grace. It can never be earned. Since we are only human and imperfect, *John 3:16* talks about the love that God has for us, and the sacrifice He made by giving His only Son's life in place of ours.

"For God so loved the world that He gave His only begotten Son that whosoever believeth in Him shall not perish but have everlasting life."

Can you ever imagine that kind of love? Would anybody you know ever sacrifice their son or child for you? Imagine the love for someone that you would do this. This is an unconditional love for all of those He created. No matter what we have done in our lives, He still loves us. He never looks at us for our faults. He loves sinners the same as He loves believers. His love is never-ending.

John 3:17 "For God did not send His son into the world to condemn the world, but that the world through Him, might be saved."

He never sent Jesus to condemn us, but to teach us about the many things we can inherit by accepting God's love. He came to teach us about His Heavenly Father so that we may come to know Him as Jesus knows Him.

We have to accept Jesus Christ as our Lord and Savior to get to Heaven. We have to truly believe in Him and the sacrifice He made for us. We cannot get to Heaven any other way. There is no back door into Heaven, only through Jesus Christ.

Does this mean if we accept Jesus as our savior we are to be perfect? No. Read *Romans 3:23.*

Romans 3:23 says *that all have sinned and fallen short of the kingdom of God.*

We have all fallen short. We can't be perfect. We weren't made to be perfect. If God had made us perfect then He could control us like robots. He doesn't want us to love Him because we are programmed to do so, He wants us to love and accept Him through our own free wills. We are not perfect. We can only strive each day to be in the will of God and work toward maturity.

Romans 5:8 states, *"that while sinners Christ died for us, that we might live with God forever".*

God chose His Son who had no sin to be sin for us, that we might become the righteousness of God in Him. This is a free gift from God. We don't have to do anything for it. He saves us through His grace. Can we remain the way we are without having to change some of the things we do? No we have to change some of the things we do and how we live but after you have accepted Jesus and become saved you want to do anything you can for God. We turn our minds off of the things of this world and turn to the things in Heaven.

1 John 4:10 states, *"In this love, not that we loved God, but that He loved us and sent His Son to be the propitiation for our sins."*

This is a tremendous love from God. He loves all of His children the same. We were saved by His grace: A free gift of salvation. He sent His Son for the propitiation of our sins. Even though Jesus had done nothing wrong He suffered all of the pain for us: **For our sins.**

Ephesians 2:8 *"For by grace you have been saved, through faith and that not of yourselves."*
We don't earn grace. God gives His grace and it is by our faith and our decision whether we accept

it or not. Without faith, it is impossible to even believe in God. We have to accept Jesus Christ by faith. We cannot earn grace through ourselves. It has to come from Him.

Romans 10:13 "Whoever calls on the Name of the Lord shall be saved."

Jesus loved you so much He died on the cross for you, so that you may have the chance to go to Heaven and sit on the right hand of the throne of God. All you have to do is ask. Call on the Name of Jesus and ask for forgiveness of your sins and He will be there, ready, willing, and able to forgive you. WHOEVER calls on His Name. He doesn't care what you have done in the past. He can forgive that; He desires for you to be saved. He doesn't care who you are. He desires for you to be saved. Call on the Name of the Lord.

Pray this prayer from the depths of your heart. You do not have to go down in front of the church to be saved. You can be saved from your own home. Be completely humble in your repentance. Know that you will be forgiven of your sins and be saved. Allow Jesus to become a part of your Spirit. Make a conscious choice to become a member in the family of God. He will hear your prayer and forgive your sins, and give you his free gift of eternal salvation.

Romans 10:13, says, ***"Whoever calls on the Name of the Lord shall be saved."***

If you have never asked Jesus Christ into your heart and be your Savior please ask Him now!

Scripture: Romans 10:13, "Whoever calls on the Name of the Lord shall be saved."

Prayer: Dear God,

Thank you for loving me so much that you gave your only Son who gave His life for me. I need your love and forgiveness for my sins and I choose right now to receive Jesus as my Lord and Savior. I believe that Jesus is the Son of God that He died on the cross for my sins, that He rose again.
I accept Your love and Your free gift of salvation as my own. Thank you Jesus for saving me. Thank you Jesus for dying on the cross for me.

In Jesus' Name,
Amen.

Now the next step is to find a church to attend, start getting in the Word and reading the Scriptures, pray and spend time in fellowship with God, and live the rest of your life as a precious child of God!

Congratulations on your decision to join the Family of God!

WORKSHEET

SALVATION

As a new believer and babe in Christ you will need to start a schedule each day to read your Bible. Start reading the Bible in the New Testament in the first book of Matthew. Read all of the New Testament before starting on the Old Testament.

Next, start a schedule to spend time in prayer with God each day. It is better if you pray first thing in the morning before starting your day. Prayer will help you to draw to a closer relationship with God.

Meditate on the Scriptures. Meditation will allow you to spend some quiet time with God for new understanding.

Tell everyone you know about your decision to accept Christ and become saved.

Choose a church your would like to attend and attend it regularly. See if they have a new believers class and join it. This will help you get off to a good start on understanding God's Word.

Ask your pastor to baptize you.

Choose to be baptized in the Holy Spirit.

NOTES

NOTES

NOTES

NOTES

www.ingramcontent.com/pod-product-compliance
Lightning Source LLC
Chambersburg PA
CBHW022023090426
42739CB00006BA/262